Memories of Home

The Writings of Alex La Guma

Edited by

CECIL ABRAHAMS

Africa World Press, Inc.

P.O. Box 1892
Trenton, New Jersey 08607

Africa World Press, Inc.

P.O. Box 1892
Trenton, New Jersey 08607

Copyright © 1991 by Africa World Press, Inc.
First Printing 1991

Cover Design by: Ife Design

Book design and typesetting by Malcolm Litchfield
This book is composed in Sabon

Library of Congress Catalog Card Number: 91-70746

ISBN: 0-86543-234-1   Cloth
         0-86543-235-X   Paper

Contents

Preface

In the early evening of Friday, October 11, 1985, Alex La Guma, one of South Africa's best known writers, suffered a fatal heart attack at his home in Havana, Cuba. At the time, La Guma was the chief representative of the African National Congress in the Caribbean. Throughout his existence, La Guma believed in the inseparability of art and life; hence his creative writing combines effectively his interest in the revolutionary struggle with his immense ability to fashion stories.

Alex La Guma was born in 1925 in Cape Town, South Africa. His father, James La Guma, was an activist in the emerging trade union movement and a member of the Central Committee of the fledgling South African Communist Party. In 1947 La Guma became a member of the Young Communist League and his career as an organizer in political activities began. When the Nationalist Party of South Africa was elected on its apartheid platform in 1948, La Guma became a full-fledged member of the Communist Party. And in 1950 when the apartheid regime outlawed the party, he was listed as a known communist under the Suppression of Communism Act.

In 1954 La Guma helped to found the South African Colored Peoples Organization (SACPO) and was elected to the executive committee. In 1955 he was elected chairman of SACPO and he led a delegation to the Congress of the People in Johannesburg. He and his delegation were prevented from getting to Johannesburg. His second brush with the South African security forces came in 1956 when he and 155 other antiracist leaders were charged with treason against the state. The trial dragged on for four years, creating disruption and hardship in the lives of the accused and their families.

From 1960 until his permanent departure from South Africa in 1966, La Guma spent several periods in detention or under house arrest. Once in Europe he continued his onslaught against the racist regime. And he also pursued his creative activities with renewed vigour. At the time of his death he had published fourteen short stories, the novels *A Walk in the Night* (1962), *And a Threefold Cord* (1964), *The Stone Country* (1967), *In the Fog of the Seasons' End* (1972) and *Time of the Butcherbird* (1979) and a host of shorter literary and critical pieces. He was busy on his autobiography and a new novel to be called *Crowns of Battle*.

In his last year several countries honored his creative and political work. The Soviet Presidium awarded La Guma the Order of Friendship; the Republic of Congo gave him the President Nguesso Literary Prize; the French Ministry of Culture awarded him the much coveted title of *Chevalier des Arts et Lettres*; and the Soviet Writers Union set aside a special evening to pay tribute to him and to celebrate the publication of a half a million copies of his collected works.

In this book La Guma's creative and political courage is celebrated through his personal remarks and memoirs from his wife and close friends, as well as an abandoned story. In this way I hope to show La Guma's remarkable strength as a socially involved person and his considerable achievement as a writer.

Cecil Abrahams
St. Catharines, Ontario

PART ONE

African Thought:
A Tribute to Alex La Guma

Dennis Brutus

By living in the
minds of others we achieve
immortality.

I knew Alex fairly well, having met him both in South Africa and Britain where we worked on anti-apartheid causes together, particularly in an effort to revive the Colored People's Congress (CPC) in exile.

I first got to know him when I visited him at his home in a segregated township called Garlandale which was part of the segregated area called Athlone.

We were different in many ways: his continuation of the activism of his radical trade union father, his involvement with trade unionist and other workers, and his association with radical journalists white and black, all these things set us apart. But we shared an interest in creative writing. It was through his association with the Nigerian journal titled *Black Orpheus* I learned of publishing possibilities outside South Africa. Later I was to read his *A Walk in the Night* published by Mbari and smuggled into South Africa. He was already banned in South Africa and it was illegal to read him.

He explained how he did his writing with one page in the typewriter and the completed pages hidden under the linoleum so that if he was raided by the police they would find only the single page in the mimeo machine and he would not have to redo the pages he had already done.

What was particularly impressive about Alex was the serious-
ness with which he approached the craft of the writer and the
intensity he gave to his work. He was determined, as a craftsman,
to do the best job that he could possibly do. This implied other
very noticeable characteristics. He made a conscious and consistent
effort to catch the quality and the rhythms of life in that particular
section of the oppressed the "colored" in which he found himself.
He was satisfied that there was a specific cultural flavor and
identity in that ethnic section of the oppressed that he belonged to.
He was proud of it and relished it, and tried to reproduce it in his
work. It explained his pleasure of sharing a bottle of cheap Cape
wine, of swapping raucous tales into the small hours of the night,
of strumming vaguely obscene and sentimental ballads or *volks-
liedjies* on a guitar while he plucked at the strings and sucked away
at a cigarette butt.

But he could swing quite suddenly into other well known
ballads as well: I enjoyed hearing him sing the ballads that Josh
White or Arlo Guthrie or Pete Seeger had made famous. He also
had a vast repertoire of the songs composed by the minstrels of
klopse of the Cape ghettos.

Because he was already banned when I got to know him well,
travelling periodically from Port Elizabeth in the Eastern Cape to
where he lived in the Western Cape, it was his wife Blanche, a
midwife, who I got to know better. She served with me on a
planning committee which was building a national convention of
the colored section of the oppressed which was to meet in October
1961 to draft an alternative constitution to the apartheid Constitution. Thus, I saw much more of her in the course of meetings. Alex
was forced onto the sidelines because of his banning orders and
fretted over this; but it was also the period when he was probably
at his most creative.

From this period and from his acquaintance with George
Peake, who spent time with him in the Colored Peoples Congress

and who spent time breaking stones with me and subsequently committed suicide in Britain, comes the material which he was to incorporate in subsequent books such as *The Stone Country*, *And a Three-Fold Cord*, and *In the Fog of the Seasons' End*.

Alex La Guma was an artist of enormous talent. He was also a man of great warmth and humanity. All his friends will remember him for his openness, his friendliness, and his easy charm. But he was also a man of uncompromising frankness. His dedication to the struggle for freedom and justice in South Africa made him blunt in his opposition to racism or oppression and forthright in his commitment to a free South Africa. He put his talent as he put his life, at the service of the struggle for freedom in South Africa.

We will remember with gratitude his contribution to the struggle.

Alex La Guma:
A Wife's Memory

Blanche La Guma

A lex and I were at high school together. Being older than I, he was two classes ahead of me. My brother and he were in the same standard, and the two of them became close friends. Alex occasionally visited my brother at our home. At that time, however, I was not interested in him, neither did he show interest in me. He probably found other interests, and came less to our house, until he stopped coming. Some years later, I found myself in the same social clubs as Alex, and we often saw each other. At this time, he showed some interest in me, and I in him, but neither was serious. Alex was interested and participated in politics since his youth. In this regard he was largely influenced by his father. In 1950 I entered the nursing profession and living-in at the hospital I did not see Alex till some years later.

One day, I walked down one of the main streets of Cape Town, while off-duty, to do shopping. Here I unexpectedly met Alex. We were both pleasantly surprised to see each other and exchanged inquiries about each other's welfare. I then learned that after matriculating he decided to get a taste of life as an industrial worker rather than to enter university. When I met him he was working in the art department of the Caltex oil company in Cape Town. While working he took a correspondence course in journalism, which was to serve him well in the future. We chatted for such a long time that I did not reach the shops. I did not mind, for I preferred talking with him rather than shopping. Having to return to work, I had to break off the conversation, but before leaving he asked when he could see me again, and I replied, "I suppose we'll bump into each other sometime as we did today." He then told me he should prefer something better than that, and asked me to afternoon tea at his home, the next Sunday. Having to be on duty that Sunday, we arranged to meet the following Sunday.

I was not aware that a further very pleasant surprise was awaiting me that afternoon at his home. Half an hour after being with him, he proposed marriage, and I accepted. We were married in November 1954 and our parents played a big role in starting us off on a long and happy partnership.

Having been at the hospital where meals were prepared and served, I had no idea about cooking. It was only when I produced the first dish that I realized I would have to learn to cook. The dried beans stew was so dry that we both nearly choked. I nudged him with my elbow and said, "just eat and don't complain—I will learn in time." He gave his usual broad smile and said that's not so important, we will both cook and that he would teach me. I learned that cooking was his hobby, he had imagination and turned out the most delicious dishes.

Alex continued work at Caltex, but after some months resigned to become full-time organizer for the South African Colored People's Organization (SACPO) later called the South African Colored People's Congress (SACPC) to fall in line with the Congress Movement under the banner of the African National Congress (ANC). Later he joined the staff of a progressive newspaper called *New Age*, where he had a column called "Up My Alley," a record of the apartheid regime's actions against the Africans.

When I returned home after the conference of the Congress of the People held in Kliptown, Johannesburg, where the Freedom Charter was adopted in 1955, I learned that Alex never reached the conference, because he, with several other delegates, were arrested in Beaufort West on their way to Johannesburg, and released after the conference had ended with no charges laid. He, with several other people, had worked hard to get the demand which appeared in the Freedom Charter.

In February 1956 our first child, a son, was born. We called him Eugene and in December of that same year I returned home at 9:00 A.M. from a midwifery case for which I left home at 2:00 A.M., Alex being in bed. My mother, with whom we lived at the time, looked distraught and worried and told me that Alex had been arrested at 4:00 A.M. by the security police. I immediately phoned the lawyer, whom I was told had also been arrested. On phoning the *New Age* office, I heard that several people there had been arrested. It became known as the dawn arrests for all were picked up at 4:00 A.M. simultaneously.

I was a little later informed by phone to pack a bag for Alex, toiletries, pajamas, etc., because none of the arrestees were allowed to take anything with them. Before I left, however, the phone rang again and I was told that if I had not yet left it would be too late, because everybody arrested in Cape Town had been flown to Johannesburg by military plane. Nobody knew what was happening. The arrests took place by security police and we all knew that it was a political matter.

It emerged that he was one of the 156 men and women from all parts of South Africa arrested on a charge of high treason.

A few days before December 25, 1956, bail was granted for all arrested and they were let out of prison. Before we heard about the granting of bail, we had planned not to celebrate Christmas as Alex was not with us. But when the lawyers informed us that bail had been granted and that all arrested would be home for Christmas, we rushed madly to buy extra food and luxuries for Christmas. In Cape Town a big and lively Christmas-Eve party was arranged, to which all the detainees and other people came. We had a wonderful time.

In January 1957 the Treason Trial actually commenced. It related to the Freedom Charter. It was held in a synagogue in Pretoria and lasted more than four years. Because of lack of evidence the case was quashed and all the defendants were acquitted. What jubilation for all of us—Alex came home. While the trial was in session, when the court adjourned for one reason or another, the detainees dispersed to their homes. One such occasion was when our son Eugene had his first birthday. I had been writing to Alex, and I wrote to him everyday about the preparations I was making for Eugene's party. Little did I know that I was building up excitement in him to be at the party. Then most opportunely the court adjourned and Alex, among a carload of detainees, arrived in time for the party. It took them ten hours to drive by car from Johannesburg to Cape Town 1,000 miles away.

One night while working at his desk, with only net curtains at the window, he was fired at in an attempt on his life. The bullet grazed his skin at the back of his neck. I can still see the drops of blood trickling onto his shirt collar. When the matter was reported, the police showed no interest. Only when he received an unsigned note reading, "Sorry we missed you, will call again—The Patriots" did they come to the house to inspect the hole made by the bullet into a wall. That was two days after the event.

In April 1959 our second child, also a boy, Bartholomew (Barto), was born. In 1960 Alex was among thousands of men and women arrested under the State of Emergency. For some weeks I did not know where he was detained as the security police refused to tell us. When I was informed, I went to visit him. He inquired why I had not come before. He was not aware that a state of emergency had been proclaimed, because this happened after his arrest. As he was not allowed to take spare clothes, he looked dirty, he was unshaven and rather neglected. I was shocked to see him in this state. He was detained at the infamous Roeland Street jail. Soon after all the detainees were transferred to a prison approximately eighty miles from Cape Town, to a place called Worcester. The transfer took place on the day and time of our visit. We were refused a visit, but after much arguing with the police we were allowed to see our people, for ten minutes only, and then wave to them as they left in police vans, singing freedom songs.

After the vans had departed, we immediately started organising transport, to take us to Worcester to be in time for the afternoon visit there. Alex was delighted and surprised to see me.

The journey to Worcester took two to two and a half hours travelling through the mountains and over mountain passes. The scenes were beautiful, and it was good to see Alex even for half an hour twice a week. However, quite often we left home at dawn, but because of the breakdown of our transport, would only return home very late at night after a dangerous journey travelling through thick fog. The children would sleep when we left home and would be sleeping when we returned, being too tired to wait for the report of their father. After five months, Alex was among the last three detainees to be released in Cape Town from the Worcester prison, without being charged. Those three were involved in the treason trial. On this last day we were refused a visit and we did not know why. When we were told that they were being released, we were still insistent about our rights and had a short visit. Eventually we went home with our husbands. Across the street and against our house, were large banners, welcoming Alex home. He was very popular and well loved in our community, and our neighbors had prepared the banners in preparation for his release. A phone call informed them of the homecoming.

In 1961 Alex, among others, campaigned against South Africa becoming a white republic. He went underground to campaign clandestinely for a national general strike, called for by Nelson Mandela. I did not know where he was over this period. Every night I was visited by members of the security police who visited our house and wanted to know where to find him. I received anonymous telephone calls at midnight telling me that my husband was dead, or that he had just been killed or that my children would be kidnapped. After the successful strike, Alex returned home, and the next day went to work. During the afternoon I received a call from one of his workmates, inquiring about Alex and who informed me that there had been arrests—when I told him that Alex had gone to work. Well, on telephoning the Caledon Square Police Station in the city, I found that Alex had been arrested in the street while on his way to work, and was being detained there. I took the prepared bag with toiletries and his pajamas and proceeded to see Alex, buying food for him on the way there. It was over this period that the twelve-day detention started, for the detainees were transferred to the Pollsmoor Prison and kept for periods of twelve days till they were eventually released without being charged.

Alex's first book, *A Walk in the Night*, was posted to Nigeria in 1960. Fortunately it was sent under registered post. When after a year the book had not reached its destination, I made enquiries at the post office. Two weeks later the book arrived back at our house. It had not been posted from South Africa. Alex's movements were restricted through banning in August of 1961. In 1962, he was the first person to be placed under twenty-four hour house arrest. He did most of his writing over this period.

One day in October of 1963 Eugene and Barto returned home from school to find the house in chaos, and both their parents gone to prison. This was particularly awful for in the past only their father was taken and I was able to be with them. They stayed with one granny during the week and with the other granny at weekends. Just before being arrested, the La Guma home was raided for banned literature for four hours and eventually, the drawers of cupboards were carried out for scrutinisation at the police station. Alex and I were detained, under the ninety-day solitary confinement clause. I knew that Alex was being detained at the same prison as I was, for he sang back in reply to songs that I sang, like light opera, the songs which we sang at home. I was released before Alex and banned. On his release, Alex returned to house arrest, and I received permission to live with Alex, since banned people cannot associate.

In 1966 Alex was again arrested under the 180-days solitary confinement clause. I had to have good reasons to leave my magisterial district to visit Alex. On one occasion Alex's mother had undergone major surgery and I used this as a means for a visit. Before permission was granted the authorities inquired whether I was telling the truth. On another occasion I asked permission to take Eugene to the clinic in the city, for orthodontic treatment. Without asking to visit Alex I was given permission to go to the clinic and permission to visit Alex on the same day and at the same time. That evening I received a visit from the security police who asked how I was able to be at two places at the same time. They showed surprise when I told them that my mother took Eugene to the clinic. They warned that my mother could also be banned. It became very clear that it was not the magistrate giving permission, but the security police.

On previous visits to Alex in prison, we were separated by a space of about four feet, with ceiling-high meshed wire on both sides, and everybody shouting conversations to each other. One could not hear what was being said. In 1966, I saw Alex in a room, with a police manipulating recording equipment, again a space of about four feet, but no wire separating. We had to speak loudly, so that the recorder could pick up our conversation. With police at the window and police at the door, we could only speak about family matters.

On his release from prison he decided to leave South Africa with us to live in exile in London. While in South Africa, in London, and in Cuba where he was later posted to become chief representative of the African National Congress, to cover the area of the Caribbean, Central and Latin America Alex and I sometimes chatted through the night talking, reminiscing and laughing. He was not a 9:00 A.M. to 5:00 P.M. writer, but wrote as the ideas flowed into his head. Some nights I would awake in the dead of night to the clatter of his typewriter.

The phrases which assisted him in his work and life were: 1) to have a sense of humor; 2) to have some knowledge of history; and 3) to have a spirit of adventure.

Eugene, Barto and I have good memories of Alex, and his

grandchildren adored him. If he had finished his last book, it would have been dedicated to his grandchildren James and William.

The Real Picture

Interview with Cecil Abrahams

In this chapter, Alex La Guma provides an intimate portrait of his growing years in the 1920s and 1930s, his years as a factory and political organizer from the 1940s onward, and the development of his writing career. We learn of his poor but intimate family life, and of parents who gave their son the encouragement to develop his own political and creative life.

At the age of eight, La Guma experiences racism for the first time at a segregated circus. This incident leaves an indelible mark on him, because as he grows older he becomes active with organizations such as the South African Communist Party and the African National Congress. When apartheid is introduced in 1948, La Guma is twenty-three years old. The regime soon begins to harass him and in 1956 he is charged with treason. Although he and one hundred and fifty-five others are acquitted in 1960, he is constantly banned and detained by the regime, so that in 1966 he and his wife, Blanche, and sons Eugene and Barto leave South Africa for exile in London and later Havana.

La Guma discusses the development of his writing career which begins formally in 1955 as a journalist first, and then from 1957 to 1985 as a short story writer, essayist and novelist. He spends some time discussing literary and political influences, and he completes the chapter with insights into his novels *A Walk in the Night* (1962), *And a Threefold Cord* (1964), *The Stone Country* (1967), *In the Fog of the Seasons' End (1972)*, and *Time of the Butcherbird* (1979).

I was born on February 20, 1925. My mother worked in a cigarette factory in Cape Town. My father at that time was a trade union organizer and he was working for the Industrial and Commercial Workers Union. The general family life was dominated by our struggle to survive on the very mean earnings which a trade union organizer of that day gained from work, and on the other hand, by the atmosphere of working-class activity, politics and ideas. I remember when I was seven years old, when my father was arrested and he was in jail for ten days for leading a strike or being involved in a strike. My mother took me up to the prison to meet him when he came out. By then my father had grown a beard during his time in prison and I was wondering who this man was. Only when he shaved himself did I see it was my father.

I went to school up on the hill above Cape Town. Most of my friends came from among my school mates. They all lived in the area of 66th and Upper Constitution Street area. All my early adventures centered around that area and among those youngsters. I must say that very often when I reminisce they all come back to my memory. I think that there are a number of them still alive today and doing one thing or another back in South Africa. I remember a particular boyfriend of mine, Daniel. He lived just opposite my home. He was of African color, in those days there was no sort of formal segregation or apartheid. People in the working-class areas lived mixed up, Africans, colored people, Indians. Anyway, Daniel was an African boy of my own age and we were great chums and he was a great favorite of mine because he was a cheerful, lighthearted fellow and we spent a lot of time as children together and then with the development of residential segregation they had to move out. His parents moved to Langa, which is just outside of Cape Town. And it was the last I saw of Daniel for many, many years and then suddenly one day when I was grown up, working, earning a living, I met Daniel again. He was not the same Daniel I had known before. He had become a gangster, been to prison and his whole life before him didn't hold any sort of rosy prospects. It was quite a moving, touching experience for me to meet him again—an old school chap who had become a victim of the circumstances which he couldn't cope with.

My first experience with racial discrimination came when I was about seven or eight years old when my mother took me to the circus for the first time. Anyway, the circus was on, it was very exciting, and when we were in the big top watching the performance I discovered that I couldn't see anything that was going on in the ring. For some reason or another the performers were always looking the other way, performing in the other direction. And I asked my mother why this was so and she told me we were sitting in the seats for black people and the main concentration of the circus was on the white audience, so we just had to take our chance with the entertainment being provided. That was the first and last time I ever went to a circus in South Africa. The next time I attended a circus was in Europe as an exile, and at that time I reflected back with a certain amount of sadness over that first situation, my first experience with racial discrimination.

I went through the usual period of primary school and then high school. I remember my principal at Upper Ashley, Mrs. Peterson. A very strict, severe and nevertheless kind woman, who intended to make sure that we would all grow up into decent and honest citizens. Afterwards I attended Trafalgar High School. Anyway, I think high school was a very awkward period for me because the rise of fascism in Europe was then taking place and the impending Second World War and I suppose from the background that I'd come from these things seemed to interest me more than sort of formal education. I was more interested in the Spanish Civil War and its progress than what I was expected to be [interested in at] school. And then again when the Second World War broke out in 1939 I was more interested in seeing the defeat of Nazism than I was in examinations and in fact I even ran away from home to join the army. But I was fifteen years old and very skinny and the recruiting sergeant just gave me one look and told me to clear off.

I think it was a bit of a difficult period so that I really didn't complete high school. I went as far as matriculation and then quit and then I passed examinations at the technical college afterwards. But the whole atmosphere was not conducive as far as I was concerned to formal education. So having finished the exams I decided first to find out what it was to be a worker, a member of the proletariat, as I romantically imagined in those times, so I went to work in a factory manufacturing tin cans and suchlike products.

Well I worked there for about a year or eighteen months and then I became involved in organizing a trade union in the factory and there were rumblings of strike action. A lot of us who were on the strike committee or union committee were sort of gently eased out of the industry. So then I worked at keeping books for a few traders. Then I worked for an oil company in Cape Town. I wasn't sort of directly involved in any political activity, I sort of followed what was going on. I read a lot, since early childhood I was always looking for books, the usual things that little children read: Stevenson, Victor Hugo. Adventure stories, westerns, and I suppose I gradually began turning towards the more serious classics, Shakespeare, the Russian authors, Tolstoy, Gorky, the American authors, James T. Farrell, Steinbeck and Hemingway. And whenever I could lay my hands on a book I took the opportunity.

My father had a great deal to do with molding my philosophical and political outlook and guiding me towards serious works, both political and cultural. He himself was an avid reader, and I suppose this had something to do with my development one way or the other. My father died in 1961, that was just before my first novel came out, *A Walk in the Night*. I suppose one could say that he didn't see the fruits of his encouragement.

My father had no formal education to speak of, he passed and he was apprenticed as a shoemaker. Most of his education he gained by his own efforts at reading and so on. I have done a short biography of my father, it is still in manuscript form.

My mother was concentrating mainly on keeping us from dying of starvation. She was concerned, like all mothers, with food, clothes and so on. And so that in that way she certainly had some influence on my upbringing. I have a sister who is living in South Africa in Cape Town at the moment. She is eight years younger than I am. She is married to a building worker and she herself is a teacher.

I don't know when I really started to become interested in writing. I do remember as a child, as a schoolboy putting pen to paper. On a couple of occasions I produced essays in school which were read out to the class. It didn't strike me as being the gems of authorship, but teachers said I had a certain talent for writing. I used to concoct stories which were, well, the kind a schoolboy would write—schoolboy adventures, and filling in exercise books which mounted up at home. And I remember in the spring time when I would have to throw all these valuable manuscripts in the garbage.

I touched on literature for the first time when I was asked to join the staff of the *New Age* newspaper in Cape Town. That was in 1955. Well before then I had done a couple of pieces for the old *Guardian*. *New Age* was looking for staff from among the black community then. They asked me to take a job and that is when I really started to write seriously. I worked as a reporter at *New Age* until 1962. I also produced a column of mostly satirical, humorous observations for the paper and I suppose, inevitably, I sat down and wrote short stories. I also wrote for the magazine *Fighting Talk*, and once or twice for *Africa South*, and I submitted a story to *Drum* magazine which they ruined. I remember the first short story that received any serious consideration. I remember it was called "Out of Darkness," which appeared in *Africa South*. Then another called "Nocturne." Well, since then I have been carrying on.

Having read South African literature, I have discovered that nothing satisfactory or worthwhile from my point of view had been written about the area from which I sprang. So I think there was a conscious effort on my part to place on record the life in the poor areas, working class areas, and perhaps for that reason most of my work is centered around that community and life.

I think that there is a very wide and vast stage, and many

performances can take place on the stage, but if we want to make the play really representative of the subject then we have to draw in all the scenes which can give the picture. And certainly the African majority provides the most important aspect of South African life, but I think that the future culture of South Africa or what we hope will be called the South African culture will be made up of contributions from the other communities as well. So that we have to, at this time, give an idea of what the real picture is and encourage the various communities to draw closer towards contributing to this broader cultural life that we are looking forward to.

I don't think that one goes around saying that the aim of the writer should be to do this or to do that. A writer, if he is conscious of what is going on around him, automatically reflects this picture, this scene, and through portraying the life around him also produces his own ideas about it. Of course, what should be borne in mind is that a writer *is* supposed to be conscious of the direction in which his works are going to point. When we talk about the role of a writer we talk about it in terms of duty, which perhaps in ancient times the priests and magicians or so-called shamans used to perform in terms of guiding a community. I presume that the talented members of society who are writers have this duty, although in modern times a lot of these things have been forgotten. In any event, so that when we speak of the role of the writer and I think that it is the role of the conscious writer to guide the morals, the perspectives and the objectives of the community. The community might be small, depending upon his own outlook; the community can be national, and the community can be universal. All this depends to what extent the writer's consciousness embraces the things which influence not only himself, but all people.

In South Africa, inevitably, writers are going to be concerned with the race situation. In a way, inevitably, because that is the life of South Africa, and I think that even the most innocuous writings of South Africa in one way or another reflect the specter of race in South Africa; even unconsciously on the part of the writer. If we read some book used in school, a novel about life on the farm, even that reflects a race situation because you always have some black servant who is at least on the farm or he was a very faithful retainer, serving his master with diligence, all these are aspects of South African life. The black writer, who is more conscious of being part of the community in terms of social, economic and political situations has to reflect the racial problems in South Africa. Being first of all a black writer, he is going to protest against racism. And from protest, he can also demand change. When you said his "aim," I don't think it is a sort of a conscious aim but is an inevitability in South Africa. The conscious aim comes more from those white writers who have now decided that they too must protest apartheid. I think with us it is more of an inevitability rather than an aim. It is a way of life with us.

I decided that nothing had been said about my community, and I placed on the record what I believed should have been there. This I believe is part of my function as an historian of the people. Apart from that you notice that my work is concerned with resistance, active resistance to the situation in South Africa. Well, this is also part of the writing of the history of a people.

I can't think of any particular writer who really influenced me in terms of my outlook or my ideas, perhaps their influences of style or technique and so on, but I wouldn't say that such and such a writer made such an impression on me. The other day I was asked to write a short note on how Tolstoy had influenced me. Well, I could write what I thought of Tolstoy, but Tolstoy did not influence me because I read his books and that's it. I cannot say that in such a time Tolstoy made such an impression on me that I wanted to imitate him or be like him. No, I don't think there was any specific writer. I think I turn towards socially conscious writers in general. There were times when Steinbeck produced works which were related to things which I was interested in terms of social problems and so on. So there were other writers and from this point of view of course one can say why not one more than the other, but to say that any particular school of writing I went through made some impression—no. It is quite possible, but I can't myself say which one of them was the most influential.

I have been talking about our community; our community culturally has been Europeanized. We speak European languages. Our cultural background is European as a result of the colonialization of the Cape province in particular. And because we read and write English, we tend to those authors for our education. So to that extent I suppose European, particularly the English language writers, have influenced me because that is the circumstance of South Africa.

I remember when I was a little boy, we used to get on the street corners under the street lamp and it was always my job to tell a story, and I used to concoct out of my imagination some kind of adventure, which children are fond of listening to. Well, I suppose these might have been the first signs of talent but which I never really bothered about. Well, I suppose also you know growing up at a certain stage in our social history there was really no demand and no opening for creative literature at that time. You know I think that the real serious writing from the blacks in South Africa really came in the 1960s, after the Second World War when there was the emergence of these newspapers and magazines for black people, and there was a demand for writers to produce work. Before this, there was a sort of obscure flower blossoming among the weeds.

Certainly I would want all my work to be read in South Africa because I believe that the work concerns the South African people, and it is a disappointment, of course, [that my books are banned there], but on the other hand, I also have to teach other people apart from South Africans, and I hope that the international audience learns something from these works and gets something from these works and gets some idea of what life in South Africa is about. So I am satisfied in that, the work has been translated into eleven languages, so that means more communities get an idea of what South Africa is all about.

A Walk in the Night came about when I read in the newspapers, just a short paragraph, that a so-called hooligan had died in the police van after having been shot in District Six. I didn't investigate this at all. I just thought to myself how could this fellow have been shot and could have died in the police van. What happened to him? And so I sort of created the picture, fictitiously, but in relation to what I thought of life in District Six. And so I wrote that sad story, *A Walk in the Night*. This is how *A Walk in the Night* evolved. My interpretation, my own portrayal of this incident. It could have been the result of other incidents.

In South Africa we live with the police, I believe. Black people are continually being harassed by the police. If it is not from the pass laws among the African people it is for drunkenness or other social problems among other communities. If you read the statistics, you find that South Africa has one of the biggest prison populations in the world, and the police play a big part in the life of the black people of South Africa. So that when one is concerned with social situations one can't leave out the police. I am concerned with experiences in the hands of the political police. I have had some experiences myself and I have made use of these, but again in political activity, which is also an important part of South African life today, there again you cannot leave out the security police. So that I wouldn't say that I don't think that the presence of the police [in my work] is intentional, I think it is inevitable.

The Stone Country was based upon my own experiences and the experiences of other prisoners. Most of it is completely authentic, from my point of view. I even personally shared the cell with a young man.

I wouldn't say that he is me subjectively, but let's say that the character George Adams seemed to hold together all the other scenes. You see I didn't really want to make an issue of him, himself, but more of the other people in prison. But some of the experiences, some of the dialogue, relates to what I've heard and engaged in myself. I wrote *The Stone Country* in South Africa just after I had been released from detention. I spent four months in detention. I decided while the situation was fresh to produce this novel. Well I dare say there is a commonality between *The Stone Country* and all literature about prison which has come from South Africans. In any event, prisons are routinely organized worlds; you cannot write a novel without finding similarities with other novels.

I know that a great deal of my writings sprung from the political movement in South Africa because these experiences are reflected one way or another in what I write. I joined the Communist Party in 1947. I stayed with it until it was declared illegal in 1950, I think. I have been with the ANC since the 1950s—Colored People's Congress of ANC, Indian Congress and so on.

We were arrested in 1956, a big lot of us from Cape Town traveling to join people from the rest of the country. Before then we were active in organizing the Congress of the People, and I and other people were responsible for sending a very big delegation to the Congress of the People in 1955 to Johannesburg. Our activities and subsequent sponsorship of the Freedom Charter all led to our arrest. I had been working in the Congress movement at that time when this arrest took place. I myself didn't reach the Congress of the People because we were stopped on the way and held until it was all over.

The New Age continued to pay a reduced salary while we were on trial. My wife worked as a midwife, so she was the main breadwinner in our family. But apart from that we continued to work whenever we could. So that I produced this column all the time while I was sitting in court. But on the whole, of course, the circumstances were very difficult. We spent about two to three weeks in jail while bail was arranged.

And a Threefold Cord I wrote while I was in prison on Roeland Street. My attorney brought me the contract to sign for *And a Threefold Cord*. Again it was a matter of recording history or recording situation. The book was about the suburban slums which is a character of the South African scene, whether it is Soweto or Alexandra Township, Cooksbush and so on. This was just another scene in the life of the community, another facet of the picture, and I decided again that the picture of the suburban slums did not appear anywhere in South African writing, so I said well why shouldn't I do it, because it is part of our life, our scene so it should appear in the picture.

[The decision to leave South Africa in 1966] was more of a mixture of decision and requirements of political struggle. It was felt that after having spent four years under house arrest and going into the fifth year with the prospect of another five years, there was no point in remaining locked up in one's home indefinitely, one could be more constructive outside. So we came to Europe to carry on what we were doing on another front.

I would prefer to sit in South Africa and write books there. But of course the subject would not have allowed me to write books in South Africa, so as a writer I am glad that I am here able to produce all these works that I have up to now. From this point of view it is a positive aspect of being in exile. But on the other hand having left sort of under extraordinary circumstances rather than voluntarily, and the fact that one is all the time thinking of what one can produce as a writer about South Africa, one would prefer to be there.

I must make an observation about people who are judging South African literature. I believe that if the writer can no longer write about one situation he has got to go and write about another situation. He is a writer first. He is a South African writer because of circumstances, but if he is a writer with imagination he can write about other scenes, project the same ideas that he is trying to project on other stages, so to speak. So that I suppose if I become "dried up" in terms of South Africa, then if I want to continue writing then I will write about Britain, about somewhere else. I wrote a short story about the war in Vietnam. It was published in Vietnam and it was published in other anthologies. It is the writer's individual interest which comes into play. That certainly appears in all kinds of works. If the writer is interested in pursuing his talent he should be able to do it anywhere, project himself into any situation.

I have always tried to avoid idealizing the South African scene. I don't try to present a picture where all black people are good and all white people are bad. That is not a consideration at all. The effect of black and white is purely circumstantial and there are more to it than that. So that when I portray the life of South Africa I try to show it as it actually is, as people actually are, not the usual frills that make them appear to be nice and not what they are.

The novel *In the Fog of the Seasons' End* presents an attitude that we have now protested enough and that we should fight. I believe that I had set down to a certain extent anyway the protest against the situation in our country. All of us have bewailed enough although others would continue bewailing the situation. But trying to convey a picture of South Africa one must also realize that apart from people bewailing their fate, there are also people struggling against it, and that the political and revolutionary movement in South Africa was a part of the South African scene and that one way or another people have always been fighting against this situation so that the political and revolutionary movement had to appear somewhere in the picture and this is the start, which I hope *In the Fog of the Seasons' End* provided. I tried to present the underground struggle against the regime as part of the picture of South Africa.

This theme is continued in *The Time of the Butcherbird*. The book is basically about the removal of Africans to the so-called "bantustans," the clearing of all these so-called "black spots." It also portrays the resistance people have to this. But I think an important feature of this new book is that I also deal with what I call the "schizophrenic" attitude of white people. A lot of the book is about white people in South Africa. A lot of white characters who portray, I think, the attitude of white people in South Africa. The whole scene takes place in the rural areas and the urban areas, the city, so that all this takes place against the background of the familiar drought in South Africa, and the campaign to offer prayers for the easing of the drought and to bring rain. I remember being transported from one police station to the central police station by two security police detectives, and of course I make a point of listening to everybody's conversation—you see I eaves-drop—and these two guys were talking about the fact that next day would be a day of prayer for rain. The one was asking whether he was going to attend, have a day off to go to church to attend these prayers for rain. It was a very ironic situation to be in to say the least. This drought and prayers for rain and removal of the black people from their old traditional homes and the reaction of white people, the thoughts of white people, are all part of this story. It might look like a departure for me, but I don't think so, it's part of the progression of that aspect of my picture of the South African scene.

Now I have got to write a love story. I have always thought that one should always write a love story, to be a complete author. I am going to write a book for children also sometime.

I have never considered myself bound by all these formulae which have been laid down for novels. One doesn't want to say that it is a conscious reaction against colonialism, you know, cultural colonialism, but I have always in a sort of ecclesiastic way asked myself, "Why should I write a novel because Defoe estab-lished a pattern for Europe, why should I follow that pattern?"

To tell you the truth, I had never really consciously thought of producing a novel, as such, in terms of the formal structures and so on. I just started at the beginning and ended at the end. It came out that way. I suppose it is necessary to be disciplined by certain formulas but it has never been something that I have taken specific notice of. I just constructed the whole story in my mind, whether it was a short story or a long story (I don't call it a novel, I call it

a long story). Once it has been completed in my mind I sit down
to write it and then amend it, change it and so on. But in terms of
the set formulas according to which novels should be produced,
that is never really part of it. I just saw the other day a report in
something called *Black Review* which I believe is published by the
Sprocas people in South Africa. It was reported there that there has
been an upsurge in the production of plays by the black people.
They claimed that at one time [in 1974-75] there were up to
fourteen black plays circulating in South Africa. Well there has
always been the problem, of course, with production facilities and
so on and I think that the character of a production and the form
of the play would likely change with these drawbacks, but certainly
the information one gets is that the theater has developed a lot.
Well I think that plays are first of all very close to the community.
In terms of tradition it is part of the African literary scene. It draws
the audience closer to the story and to the characters. That is one
aspect of it. The other aspect of course is the political aspect. Black
publications are censored and this causes frustration for writers and
discourages them. For the same reason I suppose there is a lot of
poetry going around, it is able to circumvent the censorship and
control of the regime. For this reason I think that the people tend,
these days, to popular kinds of participation such as plays.

I have no doubt that African writing has as an important a
place in world literature as the old works that have been produced
over the centuries by Europe and later by the Americans. I suppose
it is one of the results of the decolonializing period in that African
literature is now being seen as something to be reckoned with. And
at the same time I am sure that with the development or emergence
of African literature there will also be the emergence of African
critics. Not because they are African and they might know more
about the subject but because it is an inevitable development of
literature. And certainly it would be at the same time an asset to
the African literary scene that experts can come from the indigenous peoples, who at least have something to say about what has

been written and what should be written. So that I believe that we will see African literary intellectual development along with the emergence of creative writing.

PART TWO

Memories of Home

La Guma remembers in this chapter the inner-city district where he began his life. He describes the slum-like conditions of his neighborhood, where unscrupulous landlords greedily took the rent but did not repair the ramshackled dwellings. He takes us into his own home where his parents are involved with labor unions and political activities. It is here where his commitment for future political action is established. La Guma discusses the years of fascism in Spain and Germany and his longing to go to war against this scourge. Once he is rejected for being too young and too skinny, he concentrates the battle against his own country where apartheid is born.

In the winter the rain came down in sheets for days on end, and when it stopped for a while a stench hung over the district, rising from blocked drains and rotting piles of rubbish. On the roofs could be seen people moving about, plugging leaks and patching holes. The landlords generally made each tenant responsible for repairs to his dwelling. We lived in a small house with a tiny backyard where we had to take our baths, where my mother hung the washing, and which opened onto a narrow and smelly lane. The odors from there in summer hardly competed with those of winter. We seemed to live in a constant atmosphere of bad smells against which my parents waged a stubborn battle interspersed with their sallies against mice and bedbugs. This seemed to be one of the regular features of life in that area of Cape Town.

My parents were of the working class but they were also politically conscious people. My mother worked in a cigarette factory, while my father was actively engaged in trade-union and political work. I do not remember my parents ever preaching to me as a child, but one was always being advised to do "something useful" or to "lead a useful life." A picture of Lenin hung in our tiny living room. Very often people came to visit and I would hover on the outskirts of the conversations, listening to chats about trade-union work, political organization, "the Party." I also had an Aunt Maggie who was a staunch member of the garment workers and a very class-conscious person. She was one of those hard-case workers who stood on the picketlines during the garment workers strike of the 1930s and pulled off her shoes to knock the scabs over the head when they tried to break the lines. She related these incidents to the family with a mixture of amusement and anger. Her husband, my Uncle Bob, named their house "Stalingrad" during the war. As a result of his work in the trade unions my father went to prison for a term, and I went to meet him when he was released. Apparently all this was part of dedicating one's self to "leading a useful life." I remember, too, that, being somewhat of a juvenile artist, I was asked to help paint posters, decorate the banners or illustrate the leaflets which my father's work demanded.

Perhaps this helped one to see a little more clearly than others what really went on around one's self. Life went on in the slums, and many succumbed. As children we enjoyed the little spots of gaiety. There was the New Year Carnival, or the weekly procession of the Salvation Army—the thumping of the big drum and the tinkle of tambourines while a horde of children, with seatless trousers, I included, pranced behind towards the barracks to the music of "Brother take the hand of brother, Marching to the promised land. . . . " In this case the "Promised Land" seemed to be a hall where they served soup to the "poor and needy" in exchange for more prayers and hymn singing. But nothing seemed to change in the slums: knife fights, gang warfare, gambling. My childhood friends disappeared into this teeming morass of bad smells, dirty alleyways and cheap liquor.

But of course there was something else, as time went on. One attended the meetings eventually, we young ones were asked to pass around the hat while the elders held forth on the platform. I was surprised to see a few of my missing school chums in the audiences, in the marches and demonstrations. We were at last doing "something useful" with our lives.

At high-school I discovered that we were being taught by politically conscious teachers. After classes we were asked to attend lectures of a "political nature." There I heard long and dull discourses about the "permanent revolution" as well as dire criticisms and outright attacks on the Soviet Union, whereas in our family we had always been taught to cherish and admire the Socialist Sixth of the World. I soon gave up attendance at these activities which also went under the guise of cultural programs.

I went through my teens in the atmosphere of anti-fascism, anti-Nazism. There was the Spanish Civil War, and then the Nazi invasion of Europe. In the factory where I worked, we manufactured metal "dixies" [containers] for the army. My fellow-workers listened with a certain curiosity to my talks relating the manufacture of metal containers for soldiers to the struggle against fascism, oppression, exploitation. I was described as "a communist," and elected to the factory trade-union committee. When later a strike was organized for better pay, the whole committee was fired. I recall a somewhat youthful talk I gave on the meaning of class struggle.

The end of the war did not mean the end of fascism in South Africa. But certainly the anti-Nazi struggle had opened the eyes and given confidence to many. In our community there was a greater interest in politics, in the national liberation movement, in the Communist Party. The struggle of the black people for liberation was developing—one had to belong, somehow. But there was something else which worried one. I recalled my childhood on the outskirts of grown-up political activists—they had been conscious people of all colors and races, but they were all held together by a common persuasion. I remembered that next door to our house had actually lived a white family. When their babies were sick, my mother was called in to help. They borrowed sugar and rice from her. They were as pressed as we were. True enough, they eventually disappeared from the district, probably to live in some "white" area. But they had actually been in our street.

After the dixie factory I worked for a big commercial firm. Apart from the usual clerks and managers there was one white person who worked as the firm's printer, producing company stationary. He was an ordinary white worker in a skilled trade, of course. He had been with the firm over twenty years, and considered himself part of the company. Yet when the company reorganized itself, this man received a circular letter (possibly one of the forms he had himself printed) bluntly informing him that his services were no longer required. He was aghast. After all these years! I remembered him staring at me, a black worker, recounting all the service he had given the company. And to my horror, he burst into tears. He had felt secure in his privileged white-worker position. Yet the company found that they could do without him. Perhaps in the back of his mind he might then have felt himself at one with us.

One was concerned with black liberation. But we had also demonstrated on behalf of people of Europe, of Spain, Germany, the horror of concentration camps and the execution of revolutionaries afar. One had to be able to be both a patriot and an internationalist. So on that basis there was only one party to turn to. It had to be the Communist Party.

To *Literary Gazette*

The *Literary Gazette* in Moscow invited Alex La Guma in 1980 to write about his work and political interests. Since 1966, La Guma was a frequent guest of the Writers Union of the Soviet Union. Not only had La Guma been a member of the Communist Party of South Africa, but his father and mentor, James La Guma, had helped to form the party and first visited the Soviet Union in 1929. La Guma's books continue to be popular in the Soviet Union, and four months before his death, a collected edition of his work was released. He was also honored by the Soviet Presidium with the Order of Friendship.

When I started to write I had a feeling that not enough had been said in the past creative writing about the character, condition and mood of the South African people. South Africa has produced a wealth of literature from among its various communities, and indeed there are probably many more manuscripts unpublished, but I suppose each writer wants to throw his own light on the subject, believing that others have failed. So I tried to fill what I thought were the gaps existing in the South African scene, even perhaps to correct what I felt certain others might have misrepresented.

My first works were about urban subjects because I felt that not much had been said about this milieu especially in terms of the poor and oppressed and struggling. There had been many short stories written but few longer works of imagination. In addition I had seen many things happen around me which had never been dealt with in South African creative writing, and I was convinced that this was real material for a writer. So I wrote about the working-class districts and the urban and suburban slums, and tried to project the people's moods and reactions to their environment and to authority, especially to racism since I was writing about my own country and people.

I hoped to portray truthfully what went on in their lives, yet at the same time to indicate the developing sense of revolt which was fermenting all the time within the communities.

Inevitably I had to say something about the conscious political movement which is, of course, a stark reality in our country. One of my novels deals with the underground resistance movement in South Africa at a particular time.

In order to portray as much as possible of the South African scene, the people of the countryside had to be dealt with at some time. The forced removals of people from so-called "black spots" in the "white" areas and the government's attempts to enforce Bantustans form one of the great social tragedies of our country, and a source of both unhappiness and resistance. The peasantry and the country-people generally have been in the midst of important struggles against this aspect of apartheid, and notably since the end of the Second World War. In addition, the brutality and callousness of white landowners towards blacks have been a feature of racism in South Africa. For this reason I had to write *Time Of The Butcherbird*.

On the whole I must say that the life and the struggles of the South African oppressed people have been a source of inspiration to conscious writers, and it is only a matter of how this wealth of material is used. This applies to the material emerging from the experiences of all racial or national communities.

In *Time Of The Butcherbird* I deal with some white characters as well as black, and with their reactions not only in confrontation with these black people, but among themselves also. A lot of books in Afrikaans have been published in South Africa. These deal in an idealistic way with the Boer or Afrikaner people, especially those inhabiting the countryside, but no mention is ever made of their true attitude towards the black people on their farms. These were the kind of books we were expected to read in school and accept as true reflections of life in the countryside.

Of course the Boers are people and not machines and in literature they have to be dealt with as humans. I tried in a small way to present my Boer characters as they are within the setting of *Time Of The Butcherbird* apart from introducing a few white urban white people as well. There is also the matter of the schism that exists between English-speaking white people and Afrikaners too, which exists in South Africa, although they more often than not united when it comes to attitudes towards black folk.

Time Of The Butcherbird was written in the course of several months, although I do not work at a particular book regularly every day. So I suppose it must have taken a few weeks. It was written while I was living in London. As a writer in exile obviously there are difficulties caused by absence from the scene. But many writers have lived in exile and have been able to produce works of value. I think the writer's imagination and sensitivity are main assets which help him to project himself into a situation where he is not physically present. Also there is his knowledge of the subject as well as his experience of the past.

The problem presented by exile is that of having to keep in touch with developments. Fortunately my continued association with the revolutionary movement helps me to follow what is going on quite intimately. As long as one avoids becoming a mere observer there should no insurmountable problem of writing. After all, there are writers who remain on the scene and who fail to produce authentic works.

All my previous novels were written while living in South Africa, mostly while under house arrest. I wrote the novel *The Stone Country* when I was released from prison after arbitrary detention without trial. The book is about life in prison experienced in the main by ordinary prisoners. Political detainees of the category in which I was are allowed no means of creative freedom.

No newspapers or books are allowed, except the Bible if it is requested. No writing material is allowed. *The Stone Country* was based on my memory of personal experience and the collective experiences of other inmates of the jail in which I was detained.

Those sentenced to terms of imprisonment by the courts are, according to law, supposed to be given the "privilege" of study and reading. In spite of what the minister of police and prisons might have said about "creative freedom" for prisoners, this regulation (The Prisons Act of 1959) states that permission to use a library or to study is "subject to the discretion of the commissioner of prisons" and that permission cannot be legally claimed.

The most serious attack against political prisoners came in November 1977 when it was announced that they would no longer be allowed to study above the high-school level. This was not only aimed at the older prisoners for whom studies had provided an invaluable outlet from the rigors and deprivations of prison life, but the authorities were also bent on assuring that the "Soweto generation" would be deprived of any mental stimulation.

Over 240 prisoners on Robben Island were high school pupils. In 1977, eighty-seven enrolled for degree courses there. At least sixty-two passed their exams. All in all 211 political prisoners were involved in studies from primary school to university when the new regulation came into effect.

In April 1979 a national campaign was launched in South Africa by the Prisoner's Education Committee to secure for all prisoners the legal right to study during imprisonment. So you see, whatever the minister might have said, there is not really "creative freedom" in his prisons.

At the moment I am living in Cuba. Obviously it is a relief to live in a free atmosphere and in a socialist country after the tensions of South Africa and the insecurity of Western Europe. Though still a developing country and a relatively embattled one at that, the revolutionary enthusiasm and staunchness of Cuba in the face of adversity, the friendliness and charm of the Cuban people, all contribute to the vast change from my previous experiences. Havana is an interesting city to be around in, and I hope to see more of the whole island—the first socialist country in the Americas.

Right now I am not working on a new book, but I am always contemplating one. I suppose when once the machinery clicks together in my mind, I shall start again. At the moment I am representative of the African National Congress in Latin America, working in and from Cuba. For this reason a lot of my time is taken up by political activities and work to strengthen solidarity between the progressive forces of this hemisphere and the fighting people of South Africa.

I do not think I am the only writer who has undertaken such tasks. After all, we remember that the late [Chilean poet] Pablo Neruda was once an ambassador for his country, and that Agostinho Neto had to bear the responsibility of being president of the Peoples Republic of Angola. Nicolas Guillen of Cuba, and her national poet at that, is very active in public and political life here in his country.

Many other writers I know are socially and politically active. As I said earlier, the advantage this provides for a creative writer is that he is actually involved in, rather than a mere observer, of the world about him.

In addition I have been elected secretary general of the Afro-Asian Writers Association. This adds to my public duties with an added international responsibility. The writers association experienced some difficulty through the sudden death of the previous secretary general [Youssef El-Sebai]. This meant that the administration was faced with the problem of transition to a new administration. The Sixth Conference which was held in Luanda, Angola, laid down the basis for new perspectives for our association.

In addition to the secretary general we have four deputy secretaries placed in respective regions of Africa and Asia, as well as a secretariat whose members will prove of assistance to these officials. From this point of view the association has a broad base. We hope that various literary activities will be organized in these various regions. I envisage that we shall arrange over the next year or two, activities in Asian countries, in the Middle East, and African countries, as well as in a socialist country of Europe.

Furthermore we have widened the association by inviting guest or associated members from outside Africa and Asia. In this way we hope to interest other progressive literary figures and organizations in the work of Afro-Asian writers.

You also know that we publish our quarterly *Lotus Magazine* which is our official organ. This is also now under new management of our friend and comrade, Ahmed Fraiz of Pakistan. We are sure that under his editorship and leadership *Lotus* will flourish and become the vehicle for uniting more and more writers of Africa and Asia under the banner of our association.

One of the issues we have to face with as more and more peoples of Africa and Asia liberate themselves, will be the question of language. At the moment *Lotus* is published in English, French and Arabic. As time goes on we might one day have to consider new editions of *Lotus*. For instance, a substantial part of liberated Africa today uses Portuguese. Who knows but that our association will have to consider seriously publications on a regular basis of that language.

May I end this interview with a few words from the world-renowned Bertold Brecht:

There are those who struggle for a day and that is good;
There are those who struggle for a year and that is better;
There are those who struggle for twenty years and that is
    better still;
And there are those who struggle all their lives and they
    are the ones we cannot do without.

Where Have All the Flowers Gone? Censorship in South Africa

La Guma gave this address first in Cuba in the early 1980s. He traces the development of increasing censorship and banning of books since the inception of the racist system of apartheid in 1948. He demonstrates how various laws have been passed to ensure that South Africans see and read only that which the government wants them to.

All laws in South Africa have been enacted to maintain the racial minority's dominance over the rest of the population, the black majority. Among the results of this situation is the conviction by the majority that it has no moral obligation to obey the laws which uphold its oppression and the denial of democratic rights. The national liberation movement led by the African National Congress exists to overturn the status quo and to institute a new democratic state for the benefit of all in the country on the basis of government based on the will of all the people. This objective, as envisaged in the Freedom Charter, which is the program of the liberation movement, includes the enactment of new laws guaranteeing all their right to speak, to organize, to meet together, to publish, to preach and worship and to educate their children. These and all other laws shall together guarantee the rule by the majority.

At the moment conditions concerning the right to speak, to publish, etc., are controlled by the white racist minority, for the perpetration of its rule and these conditions are set down in numerous enactments, often amended, dating back to the earliest years of the modern white-dominated state.

When the Nationalist Government gained power, it found a host of laws and ordinances already on the statute book providing for the application of censorship. These provisions it enforced and extended with a vigor never known previously in South Africa.

The Riotous Assemblies Act passed in 1914 has been amended several times and gives the president the power to prohibit the publication of a newspaper or document which "is calculated to endanger the feelings of hostility between European inhabitants . . . and any other section. . . . "

The Native Administration Act (1927) and amended, states that "any person who utters any words or does any act or thing whatever with intent to promote hostility between Natives and Europeans shall be guilty of an offense."

Needless to say such laws have been used only to protect the interests of the whites.

The Suppression of Communism Act (1950) and amended, gives the president the power to ban any periodical or publication which promotes the spread of communism or "Serves inter alia as a means . . . calculated to further the achievement of any of the objects of communism."

The Prison Act makes it an offense to publish any sketch or photograph of a prison or prisoner or publish "false" information, the onus being on the publisher to prove he has taken reasonable steps to verify his information. The result has been a reluctance on the part of the press to expose prison atrocities.

The law establishing segregated universities, the Extension of University Education Act (1959), forbids students at these institutions to give statements to the press.

The General Law Amendment Act (1962)—the so-called Sabotage Act—empowers the government to prohibit any person from performing any act. Thus the government has prohibited all banned people from producing any material for publication, apart from other restrictions on them. It is also an offense under this law to publish the words and statements of a banned person, even after his death. This law also gives the Minister of Interior the right to demand a deposit of R10,000 from any newspaper requiring registration, this sum to be forfeited should the paper be subsequently banned.

Other laws like the Official Secrets Act, the Defense Act, General Law Amendment Acts of 1963 and 1969, the Criminal Procedure Act 1955 and 1965, the Terrorism Act (1967), all affect in one way or another the business of publication.

The Publications and Entertainments Act of 1963 hampers the press and also prohibits the production or manufacture inside South Africa of objects deemed "undesirable" by the Publications Control Board. "Undesirable" publications or objects in terms of the act are those deemed, in whole or part, (a) indecent or obscene (b) blasphemous (c) brings any section of the people into ridicule or contempt (d) harms race relations (e) prejudices the safety of the state, the general welfare, or peace and good order.

In terms of the South African press alone the threat by such a range of laws has provoked the editor of *The Star*, South Africa's largest daily newspaper, to comment that "editing a newspaper under these conditions is like walking blindfold through a minefield."

Although the press was excluded from the Publications and Entertainments Act, this was only done on the condition of the acceptance by the press of restrictions through a self-imposed code of conduct which requires it to take cognizance of the complex racial problems of South Africa and "the general good and safety of its peoples."

According to figures of the United Nations the number of titles of books prohibited under these laws, including the Customs and Excise Act which controls importation, reached 20,000 between 1971-1974. These range from *Letters of Lenin* and other speeches of [Leonid] Brezhnev to the usual sensational or pornographic publications.

The writings of hundreds of prominent leaders of the African people including those of the late Chief Albert Luthuli and the imprisoned Nelson Mandela are prohibited under the Suppression of Communism Act. Also prohibited are the works of over a hundred exiles including many prominent writers such as Ezekiel Mphahlele, Dennis Brutus, Alex La Guma, Lewis Nkosi. The latest list of books banned since 1971, a selection of which was recently published by the United Nations Unit on Apartheid, mentions also the works of Salvador Allende, Kim Il Sung, Eldridge Cleaver, Angela Davis and Fenner Brockway. Previously of course all works by Marx, Lenin, Engels and various communist writers were prohibited and continues to be so.

Also banned are hundreds of publications from trade unions, the Socialist States and any publication which upholds racial equality or describes the struggles of the peoples against racism and colonialism. These also include the publications of the United Nations specialized agencies.

By resorting to banning of writers and censorship of numerous publications the South African government hopes to prevent the leaders of the liberation movement and other opponents of apartheid from reaching the public and to isolate the people from the antiracist sentiments of the world.

Censorship has ultimately resulted in reactions from white writers in South Africa. Firstly as a result of the cultural boycott of South Africa by overseas playwrights who have withheld their works from apartheid theater; secondly as a result of the prohibition of work by South African writers inside the country.

"South African writers and artists are engaged in a hot war with censorship," the writer Nadine Gordimer reminded South African theater in 1965. She was opposing the government plan for production of plays despite the wishes of overseas authors through the Piracy Bill.

Later, in 1968, she said in a speech at the University of Witwatersrand, that the violence done to freedom of expression by the government made South African writers "a persecuted professional group in this country.... Freedom of expression is traditionally associated with a flowering—flowering of communication of the arts. There is no denying, unfortunately, that it has withered in this country in the past twenty years. Where have all the flowers gone? You will find them between the pages of the statute book, one by one, squashed flat." Miss Gordimer's book *The Late Bourgeois World* is among those banned in South Africa.

In 1971 a number of white South African writers and artists rejected South Africa's censorship system and the Publication Control Board in particular. Their bitterness and frustration was reflected in a survey made for the Paquino Society, which is concerned with censorship in South Africa. The survey was conducted by Walter Saunders, a poet and English lecturer at the University of South Africa.

Lionel Abrahams, poet and editor, said, "South African censorship, where it pretends to be a guardian of morality and culture, is in fact a servant of prejudice and philistinism, without respect for truth or art. Where it pretends to be a guardian of our security it is nothing but the bullying skivvy of politics, guarding only our convenient ignorance about ourselves and the world."

Andre Brink, another author, said: "Our censors ... have made an invaluable contribution towards the South African image as the laughing stock of the world."

Other writers and artists who were canvassed and expressed their feelings were the Afrikaans writers Jan Rabie, W.A. de Klerk, the novelist Alan Paton, Nadine Gordimer, Stuart Cloete, the poet Michael McNamara, artists Walter Batiss, Aidron Duckworth and Neville Bubow.

When the government instituted a commission to go into amendments to the Publications and Entertainments Act, it added fuel to the fire by threatening authors unless they co-operated.

Dr. Michael McNamara of Paquino Society revealed in the *Sunday Express* of January 28, 1973, that Afrikaans authors had been pressured into accepting the pending legislation with threats that their work would never be prescribed for academic study if they lodged objections to proposed changes in the act.

Andre Brink who was also a lecturer in Afrikaans at Rhodes University in Grahamstown and winner of several literary awards, described the threat as "the lowest form of blackmail," adding "Censorship as we have it today is not there to protect Afrikaans literature, as they would like us to believe. It serves rather as a deterrent."

When Brink's own book *Kennis Van Die Aand* was banned by the Publications Control Board, Afrikaans writers of the Sestigers, a group of liberal writers committed to themes dealing with the situation in South Africa, felt this to be the beginning of the end of their group.

Jan Rabie said, however, "We will not be cowed by the conservative establishment. If it becomes impossible for us to publish our work in South Africa we will publish in Lesotho or some other country."

Mr. Daantjie Saayman, a publisher, said, "If the books [of the Sestigers] are consistently banned I will not be able to afford it. No one will be able to afford it, and that may be the end of the Sestigers as far as publication of their work is concerned."

The attacks on liberal-minded white writers have caught the attention of the South African reading public and the outside world as well. (It must be remembered, however, that printing and publication have been controlled since the inception of the white supremacist state, through the numerous laws mentioned earlier, and by the very basis of the racist state.)

The formation of the Union of South Africa in 1910 signified the further unification of the oppressive forces. The immediate task of these forces was to drive the African people from the land, thus such laws as the 1913 Land Act and the Urban Areas Act.

Hitherto the African intelligentsia and others had been able to pawn their lands and buy printing presses and locate them on their land. Small newspapers and periodicals had been produced. The immediate effect of the land laws was to deprive Africans of control or publication, leaving them at the mercy of mission-owned and white business printing establishments. Thereafter followed the numerous other enactments.

The Bantu Education Act, by bringing African schools under the direct authority of a government department, gave authority to the same department to prescribe set books for all schools in the provinces.

Apart from political works it is now becoming clear that even creative writing inside South Africa can become an offense not merely as a contravention of the Publications and Entertainments Act, but against security of the State.

In April 1974 N.P. Matsau was sentenced to five years imprisonment. Among the evidence against him was the fact that he had distributed a poem deemed likely to create hostility. Students recently on trial were also charged along the same lines, having such poems, for example, "Black Nana Avenge," published in 1963. The *Johannesburg Star* commented that this was an interesting phenomenon. It was action taken against thoughts and not deeds.

It was reported that a book of poems written by him would be used against the Afrikaans writer Breyten Breytenbach charged under the Terrorism Act, and the Suppression of Communism Act.

The attack of the cultural life of South Africa is becoming less and less a matter of censorship and more and more obviously involved in the struggle to overthrow the whole system of racism and white supremacy. For this reason it is necessary for cultural workers, writers, artists and educators to identify themselves and their works with the struggle for the liberation of South Africa from the racist yoke. A truly democratic South Africa will guarantee cultural expression for the good of all and the fostering of that humanism which is the universal character of all progressive art and literature.

Culture and Liberation

This address was given by La Guma to an Afro-Asian Writers congress in 1975 in Tashkent, Soviet Union. It has since appeared in *World Literature in English*. La Guma observes that he has been both a writer and a political activist and that he has never seen a contradiction in his position. For him, art and politics are inseparable. He goes on to illustrate this principle in the essay. Furthermore, he demonstrates how, if African people are removed from their traditional roots, their art will suffer.

The topic being presented here has been the subject of so many conferences, seminars and workshops that one's immediate reaction on being asked to reintroduce it is that there is little new to say and that all the old ideas can conveniently be repeated. It is, therefore, difficult to avoid the risk of repetition, but since the cause of art and the cause of liberation is centuries old, the inevitability of reiterating the finest principles of both is unavoidable, and in this turbulent age, their emphasis is essential. One may ask what has art, culture, literature got to do with liberation? The question is usually asked by those who wish to separate culture or art from politics, for when we talk of liberation we are talking of it also in its political sense. But life is the criterion through and by which the artist's imagery and literary observations are evaluated. When we talk of the relationship between art and life, we mean that unity between what is reflected and the manner in which it is reflected, and this is the quintessence of art.

What we respond to when we read a poem or novel is not only life, but also its artistic merit. But life does not merely mean breathing in and out, it involves also man's struggle to reach higher levels of civilization, of social, economic and cultural status, the mighty struggle to conquer his own disabilities and forces of nature. So then life must include struggle for liberation from all that hinders his development, and as we have said that life is the stimulation of artistic endeavor, art cannot be separated from this desire for liberation. The struggle of the peoples of what we sometimes call the third world for national liberation and independence has become a titanic force of man's progress and is without doubt one of the most dynamic and most important features of our time. Perhaps we might even say that for the first time man has come to realize the totality of his planet Earth; that all Earth is inhabited by man and that the principles which seemed once to be a monopoly of apparently learned metropolitan countries now apply equally to those once looked upon as lesser beings. We by no means defend imperialist rule by recognizing that by reducing the world's dimensions, it gave it greater horizons; that it revealed new phases in the development of human societies and, in spite of or as a result of prejudices, discriminations and crimes it perpetrated, it helped to impart a deeper knowledge of man as a whole, as a unit in the complex and diverse character of his development.

Indeed paying all respect to Europe, I believe that at the pass of Thermopylae where certain Spartans died for independence centuries ago, there was erected an inscription which says: All the world is the grave of heroes. Unfortunately, through historical circumstances the Philistines of Europe—ignoring the lofty principles which had risen among them since the times of ancient philosophers, forgetting the words of "La Marseillaise," the works of Heine and Goethe, the ideas of Byron—set out to plunder and subject other peoples. This was described as a civilizing mission. It is hardly a matter of question as to who were the more "civilized:" those naively friendly Indians who welcomed Columbus, the people of the Cape who met Van Riebeeck, or their European visitors who quickly returned these greetings with firepower and "the royal hunt of the sun." "A clash of cultures" it is designated: these burnings for accumulation of gold by the Inquisition; this description of Van Riebeeck's diary of the massacred and plundered local people as "a stinking nation;" this blowing from a cannon of Sepoy "mutineers," and the "civilizing" warcry, "the only good Indian is a dead one," as the prairies were seized from their owners.

In Europe herself the common people groaned under the yokes of their own slavery and the feudal system. The example of the Russian revolution released the energies of millions of people, gave them confidence in the ultimate success of their aspirations. The period after World War II in particular saw the development and success of anti-imperialist struggles, particularly in Africa and Asia. The degrees of independence might vary from country to country, but certainly major advances have been made in destroying the old colonial empires governed from Europe. The peoples of these countries are reaching towards modern forms of civilization and culture, working to end the heritage of the colonial past, to catch up what they missed during centuries of foreign oppression and to take their rightful place alongside advanced countries.

On a subject people colonial domination may be imposed by way of suppressing traditional ways of living and thinking, together with the introduction of alien ideas and values, since the essential feature of colonization is the destruction of a people's identity. This may be done through various agencies of the colonial power. The Kenyan writer, Ngugi Wa Thiong'o, in a university paper, says: "A Chinese, a Frenchman, a German or an Englishman first imbibes his national literature before attempting to take in other words. That the central taproot of his cultural nourishment should lie deep in his native soil is taken for granted. This a.b.c. of education is followed in most societies because it is demanded by the practice and experience of living and growing. Not so in Africa, the West Indies, the colonized world as a whole despite the crucial roles of the twin fields of literature and culture in making a child aware of and rediscover this environment .... The other day I found my

own son trying to memorize a poem by William Wordsworth . . . .
I asked him: 'What are daffodils?' He looked in the book: 'Oh,
they are just little fishes in a lake!' [At another school] they told us
about a poem of fourteen lines called a sonnet written by one
William Shakespeare comparing old age and winter!!"

As we tried to explain on another occasion, if many Africans
become alienated from their cultural background, if they are so
uprooted that they dare not assert it openly any longer, this
background never dies completely. It survives the death of tribal
economic structures and remains hidden, ready to be used again as
a basis for future development. The late Amilcar Cabral said: "The
exercise of imperialist domination demands cultural oppression, but
the people are able to create and develop a liberation movement
because it keeps culture alive in the teeth of organized repression
of cultural life—because its politico-military resistance being
destroyed, it continues to resist culturally." The colonial power
cannot impose a complete cultural occupation. The majority of the
people retain their identity and are the one entity really able to
preserve and create it—that is, they can make history.

A people's cultural manifestations, including their literature,
oral and written, their songs and poetry, reflect this resistance,
reflect the various stages of development of the anti-imperialist
movement. At a certain time resistance may take on various forms,
politically passive or active, economic or armed; as it develops
other political methods including violence to end imperialist
violence. Perhaps the best examples of this cultural plus political
manifestations are contained in the peotry of the former Portuguese
colonies. Investigation shows that the history of poetry of the
people of these territories for centuries under the Portuguese, is also
the history of their revolution. The liberation struggle is the most
complex expression of the people's cultural energy, of their identity,
of their dignity. Liberation opens up new avenues, helps to enrich
art and culture, and in the course of the anti-imperialist struggle
finds new forms of expression. These manifestations also become

a powerful instrument for political information and training, not only for independence but also in the great battle for progress.

What should be taken into consideration is that the anti-imperialist struggles involve the national liberation, a struggle for the consolidation of a cultural community, for national statehood, national territory, a national economy. Colonialism and its attendant manifestations prevents this process. In addition anti-imperialist struggle has united millions of people across borders and across continents. Out of the artistic manifestations of this struggle can also be traced a common desire, ambition, aspiration, that of international friendship and indeed a brotherhood, based upon equality which includes the fusion of all that is good in all cultures into the basis of an eventual common world culture. We have talked of this struggle for national liberation, of anti-imperialism. This implies of course that imperialism and its colonial system is not yet dead.

Only recently the people of Angola entered victoriously the final stages of their battle to set up an independent state. To the south of them the white minority regimes still menace and frustrate the ambitions of the peoples of Namibia, Zimbabwe and South Africa who are engaged in heroic resistance to these regimes. A quotation from *A Short History of the African National Congress* illustrates concisely the cultural basis for the national struggles of the African majority: "The most astonishing feature of that conference [in 1912] was the number of tribes who sent representatives. There were Zulus, Xhosas, Tswana, Sothos, Vendas, Shangaans, Tongas, and others. These tribes, some of them only recently locked in feuds, had looked upon others as equals. For two years before they had seen the bitter fruits of their disunion and division when at the formation of the union they had all been ignored when Boer and Briton met to form the so-called Union of South Africa. As Dr. Pixley ka Isaka Seme, prominent leader and lawyer, stated at the conference: 'We are one people. These divisions, these jealousies, are the case of all our woes and of all our backwardness and ignorance today.' And further: the ANC realized from the outset that the problems of forging unity among Africans was the *key* to our freedom struggle. The formation of the ANC therefore marked the birth of a nation whose foundation was laid in a stirring call by Dr. P. I. Seme, later to become its treasurer-general, when in an article written in 1899 he declared: 'The demon of racialism, the aberrations of Xhosa-Fingo feuds, the animosity that exists between Zulus and the Tongas, between the Basuto and every other native, must be buried and forgotten. We are one people.'"

Cabral said that culture is the dynamic synthesis, at the level of individual or community consciousness, of the material and historical reality of a society or a human group, of the relations existing between man and nature as well as among man and social categories. Clearly a multiplicity of social categories and particularly of ethnic groups makes the role of culture in the liberation movement more difficult to define, but this complexity cannot and must not lessen the importance of the movement, most of all to recognize and define the contradictory data so as to maintain the positive values and channel them in the direction of the struggle, with an added dimension—*the national dimension*. Within the indigenous society the action of the liberation movement on the cultural plain entails cultural unity, corresponding to the moral and political unity necessary for the dynamics of the struggle. With the opening up of closed groups, tribal or ethnic, racist aggressiveness tends to disappear and give way to understanding, solidarity and mutual respect, a unity in struggle and in a common destiny in the face of foreign rule. These are the sentiments which the mass of the people adopt readily if the process is not hindered by political opportunism.

South African white domination moved away from a policy of elimination or enslavement of the immediate local population to an advanced stage of capitalism and imperialism within which the black population serves as colonial serfs and a major part of the industrial working class, all within one geographical boundary. It must be observed that the attitude of the ruling power is hopelessly contradictory. On the one hand the white ruling class has to maintain divisions, a system of apparent conservation conditioned by confinement of indigenous population in geographic zones, or reserves called homelands or bantustans, to destroy the cultural unity of the African people; on the other hand to maintain its industrial enterprises, a working class contrary to ethnic or tribal divisions.

The late Dr. Verwoerd conveniently equated "tribe" with "nation" and claimed that the so-called bantu homelands established the rights of these different "nations." Mr. John E. Fobes, deputy director-general of UNESCO, stated in Paris in April 1975:

South Africa has made much of her protection of separate cultures. What does this amount to? Does this mean restoring the economic and political bases on which independent African civilizations were built? Certainly not. These were broken in a series of wars of conquest, in the introduction of wage labor and the alienation of the land. Does this mean restoring the trade routes, the cultural exchanges which archeologists now tell us existed before European conquest? Certainly not, for in the place of so-called tribes absorbing each other, constructing as did the Zulus, a coherent Kingdom, we have tribal separation. Does the South African protection of separate cultures mean what UNESCO means by the diversity of cultures? Certainly not. For the diversity of cultures implies a relative equality of power relations and the right of groups to maintain, to change, to borrow. It is for the culture groups themselves to decide the direction of evolution of their cultures. On the other hand, we have in South Africa a government-imposed "traditionalism"—in fact, the use of traditional culture to maintain the legitimacy of a culture of domination (Seminar on South Africa, UN Special Committee Against Apartheid, Paris, April 1975).

Mr. Fobes further put the matter in a nutshell: "The Republic's protection of cultures means for Africans the external trappings of once-great cultures reduced to the folk-loric and caricature." To maintain the legitimacy of a culture of domination—these words explain the white supremacists' rationalization of their fear of being culturally drowned in the sea of liberated Black cultural development. "Our culture will be obliterated" or "We shall be swamped." This, direct economics and politics apart, is the rallying cry of the white laager. It is an old pretext. Forgetting that Europe gained from mathematics, the compass and a host of cultural and scientific contributions made by those outside that continent, the racists insist that the Blacks and Asiatics have nothing to offer but a return to barbarism. A variation of "east is east and west is west, and never the twain shall meet."

It is not a digression to point out that Japan, constituting a people who prefer chopsticks to knives and forks, is today one of the great industrial nations of the world. Nearer home, we might point out that the improverished and "barbaric" black working class man the most advanced industrial enterprises, manifestations of "Western" culture in modern South Africa. The preservation of "our culture," the "clash" of cultures are old cliches which, consciously or unconsciously, racists have mouthed for latter centuries in order to preserve a system of economic exploitation and deliberate subjugation of so-called inferior peoples.

We say "latter centuries" because contrary to the belief that racial prejudicial ways existed, racism is a phenomenon of capitalism and did not exist as a social phenomenon before the advent of this system. The slaves of ancient Greece and Rome knew of no difference in their masters' attitude to them dictated by their outward appearance. The white gladiator, Spartacus, received the same treatment, took the same risks as the gladiator for Africa.

Moslems were received into the Christian or Jewish religions in the Middle Ages, and vice versa, without consideration of racial origin; religious differences were the main ideological reasons for overrunning alien lands in the epoch of feudalism.

The development of the plantation system and production for profit gave rise to the slave trade. Africa became the main source of supply. At first the plantation owners and traders were content to claim that slavery was essential for the nation's economic prosperity. Later when the opponents of slavery stepped up their opposition, the idea was propagated that blacks were inferior beings with no sense of morality, they were apes, they had no souls. Racism became a characteristic in the ideology of exploitation since these times. Thus it is doubly easy for the "embattled" white minority "defending" their culture from the majority black "hordes" to claim that they fulfil a "God-given mission" on the tip of Africa, defending "civilization against barbarism."

Inevitably the false logic of a "superior" race or culture must contract upon itself. Thus Naziism included the conception of "pure Aryan Germans." In the same way this "logic" has given rise to the South African racists' bigoted and intolerant attitude towards cultures even within their own race. The study for the UN Unit on Apartheid, "White Immigration to Southern Africa," points out: "Intending immigrants are asked to state their religion .... [Towards the end] of the 1960s there were many Afrikaner protests about numbers of people arriving from Southern Europe—Portugal, Spain, Italy, Greece.... Thus the Nasionale Jeugbond (Nationalist Youth) expressed fear that the large number of immigrants threatened the identity of the Afrikaner, calling for a policy of immigration 'which will not endanger the future of the Afrikaner nation.' A delegate to a Transvaal Nationalist Party Congress protested, 'Colored people cannot marry my daughter, but when she is twenty-one a Portuguese can.'"

The dynamism of the developing revolutionary situation in South Africa will inspire the genuine cultural manifestations of our people, through their artists, writers, poets, black and white. Our art and culture, as someone stated elsewhere, will be warmed by the fires of the battle for liberty. As this struggle develops the people's art, as we have pointed out in the case of the former Portuguese territories, will reflect our struggle. Revolutionary poetry is today used in evidence against students arrested for opposing the South African regime; academics, black and white, are getting arrested for identifying themselves with the struggle for liberation. Drawn by the lodestone of the people's struggle, those who unhappily have had to accept the ruling power's cultural colonization in segregated universities, fed on the crumbs of so-called bantu education, are forming part of the people's wide movement for national liberation.

Southern Africa today is rapidly developing a revolutionary situation which can turn the tide once and for all in favour of genuine democracy and progress. The heroic examples of Mozambique and Angola have raised the hopes and spirits of millions still ruled by the barbarian vandals represented by the white minority racists. As we have tried to point out earlier, the anticolonialist struggle has drawn millions of people together from all parts of the world. The colonized countries, the newly independent countries, the progressive, enlightened people of the metropolitan countries, the socialist world, all form this mighty force, reinforcing each other in the struggle for the progress of all mankind. South Africa has no longer become a localized issue.

> The oppressed people of South Africa ... have committed themselves to the struggle to recover their legitimate rights in accordance with the Universal Declaration of Human Rights. ... The entire world, the international community and all international gatherings have recognized that ... it was vital to help the liberation movement in this duty of liberation. Today, more than in the past, this assistance has become a necessity. It must be multifaceted: political,

diplomatic, cultural, economic and material (OAU Executive Secretary Dramane Ouatarra, to the United Nations).

While the success of the national liberation movement unites all sections and ethnic groups of a people under the banner of nationalism, and it accelerates the process of nationhood; while cultural manifestations will reflect this fusion in terms of national art, national literature and so on, the influence of the international character of the struggle at the same time gives the national forum an international content.

Other things apart, this depends also on whether the liberation movement establishes the precise objectives to be achieved on the way to regaining the right of the people it presents and whom it is assisting to make its own history, to control freely the disposal of its productive forces, with an end to the eventual development of a richer culture—popular, scientific and universal. The South African racists wish to maintain the African people, and indeed the whites themselves, within the narrow confines of a "traditionalist" past. But the advances of the twentieth century cannot entertain the anachronisms of stultifying tribalism and "laagerism," inevitable as their doom may be. Culture is closely linked with economic and social reality, with the levels of productive forces and the methods of production in society in which it struggles and flourishes. So it is obvious that the oppressed once liberated must make use of the advances made within society, now withheld from them, in order to advance themselves.

The main concept of the struggle in South Africa today is the liberation of the African majority. At the same time, the program of the liberation struggle states that South Africa belongs to all who live in it, black and white; that the wealth and the development of such resources shall not be manipulated by any one group or individual. The revolutionary program of the African National Congress with which this writer identifies, states: "A democratic government of the people shall ensure that all national groups have equal rights, as such, to achieve their destiny in a united South Africa." Given equality, the universal and inevitable cultural exchanges with mutual respect will lead eventually to the emergence of the aforementioned richer, popular, and universal character of the South African people.

In conclusion, let us hear again the words of Nelson Mandela at the Rivonia trial which resulted in his imprisonment for life:

> In their relationship with us, South African whites regard it as fair and just to pursue policies which have outraged the conscience of mankind and of honest and upright men throughout the civilized world. They suppress our aspirations, bar our way to freedom, and deny us opportunities to promote our moral and material progress, to secure ourselves from fear and want. All the good things of life are reserved for the white folk and we Blacks are expected to nourish our bodies with such pieces of food as drop from the tables of men with white skins. This the white man's standard of justice and fairness. Herein lies his conception of ethics. Whatever he himself may say in his defense, the white man's moral standards in this country must be judged by the extent to which he has condemned the vast majority of its inhabitants to serfdom and inferiority.
>
> We, on the other hand, regard the struggle against color discrimination and for the pursuit of freedom and happiness as the highest aspiration of all men.

Has Art Failed in South Africa?

Alex La Guma's mind was frequently occupied with the question of art, and, in particular, with the kind of art that apartheid South Africa produced. In this particular piece, written in the late 1970s, La Guma responds to the white South African painter, Cecil Skotnes, who complained about the depth and authenticity of the visual arts in South Africa. La Guma agrees with Skotnes that although South Africa is blessed with beautiful scenery and interesting, intriguing and complex communities, the art produced in South Africa is rather timid, drab and uninteresting. La Guma is especially critical of the white artists because in their work he finds a tendency towards escapism.

The rolling veld, the karroo in spring, still-lives of wild flowers and the majesty of the Drakensberg Mountains, these are the subjects chosen by many South African painters, and they decorate the houses of the well-to-do or are lined up in various art galleries.

It is concentration on this aspect of the South African scene which has compelled the painter Cecil Skotnes to comment (*Rand Daily Mail*, November 3, 1976) on "a singular lack of guts" in South African art. "Since the high days of the little Bushman who set down a complete document of his lifestyle, no school of art or period has ever attempted to come to terms with what we call 'South African'," he says.

Skotnes observes that South Africa at present is embroiled in "a classic revolutionary situation" and that the stimulation arising from this situation should affect all the elements of the creative society and in particular the artist. "In South Africa there is a small bright light pointing the direction we must travel. The main artistic contribution of that direction has been made by our writers ... they have written without fear and sometimes at great personal discomfort. From Plaatjes, Gordimer and Fugard, from Eglington to Grey, the accent has always been man and his living in our sun-kissed land. Not so in painting and sculpture."

Putting aside censorship and the practice of apartheid, reading is of course among the most popular cultural pursuits of the people. They can go to libraries, buy from second-hand stalls and bookshops, but it is only the rich who can afford to purchase individual works of fine art, and the ruling minority prefers not to have its walls hung with reminders of the oppressive society it perpetrates. In addition to the ideological influence of the ruling clique, the painter and sculptor is also bound to consider the home market while the writer often has the chance of selling his work abroad.

In more open class societies art for the general populace has to a certain extent gained ground. One can, for instance, name places like Mexico where gigantic public murals of Rivera and Orozco are on view. In the socialist countries a point is made of orientating art towards the political and cultural upliftment of the common folk.

Certainly over the years South Africa has produced individual artists who have demonstrated various degrees of social consciousness and we are reminded of such as Peter Clark, Lesley, Gerard Sekoto, Feinberg, Dumile Feni, but Cecil Skotnes is commenting on the sum of fine art in South Africa.

It was once remarked by an overseas observer that white South Africa has not produced one painter of international repute, no singer, opera or ballet company. Neither, one can say, had Nazi Germany. It is not necessary to dwell on the cultural poverty of racist and fascist minorities, but these are phenomena of capitalism, a class society, and it is in this type of society that we find the emergence of two cultural expressions: that of the upper class and that of the oppressed.

Mr. Skotnes laments that "since the British decided to do away with the last vestige of the Zulu empire in 1879 to further the aims of the great imperial family, the systematic application of Western culture has destroyed those tribal forms which might have created a folk art of consequence."

For us "the systematic application of Western culture" also means the development of capitalism in South Africa, but far from attempting to turn the clock back to mourning and destruction of tribal forms, it should be realized that the process, together with the emergence of the national movement of the blacks, also welded the various ethnic groups into a vast working class and a united African people. The cultural expression of this force in South African society, in spite of attempts to divide it, consequently transcends the more ethnic or folkloric. Here we must also question Mr. Skotnes' knowledge of the history of the African people when he asserts that there is "on the black front the lack of a strong artistic tradition." If as Cecil Skotnes goes on to say, "the almost total disregard for the visual arts by the indigenous people is perhaps the greatest loss," it it not their fault, but that of a system which has little regard for culture and denies a population the stability and security in which such as the plastic arts can flourish. For this reason, among others, the oppressed people have concentrated on other art forms: songs, poetry and writing. While Cecil Skotnes might claim that the "vast urban complexes such as Soweto develop without any consideration for the artistic potential of the black man" we need not agree that it "weakens the artistic power of the whole nation," for the people continue to manifest a cultural life.

What should be expected from the present revolutionary situation, Skotnes states, is a "meaningful artistic upsurge and an intensification of output although it must be realized that what finally emerges might well be mediocre in quality." Again we do not agree that mediocrity is the result of artistic commitment to or involvement with a revolutionary upsurge. Mr. Skotnes' view is perhaps echoed by the poet Uys Krige (who, incidentally, we understand fought for the Spanish Republic in the Civil War) who said in the *Johannesburg Star* (November 9, 1976): "The poet's job is to express what is lasting and abiding, what is common to all people. The closer you get to the politics of your times, the more insignificant you become."

Revolutionary situations and revolutions themselves unleash the vast cultural potential of the common people and great works of art and literature by individual artists have been inspired by such upheavals in society. We do not wish to repeat all the discussions on this theme which have appeared before in this journal, but it is worthwhile reiterating that for the artist to ignore social realities is no guarantee that he will produce works of merit.

Mr. Skotnes nevertheless longs for "effective contact between the various fragments of the 'art world'" which he rightly says "has been blocked not only by government decree but more so by the vast difference in living standards between the overfed whites and the underfed blacks. This applies to intellectual pursuits as well as food," and acknowledges that "the blacks, after all, control the final outcome of the present confrontation of ideas." His complaint is that the divisions which exist in South Africa, and the destruction of "trivial forms" and "folk art" did away with "a foundation on which to build an identifiable expression," perhaps a unified art. This is also ignored by artists who go on demonstrating the "lack of guts" by producing "'good' pictures" that have "... little to do with humanity and atmosphere of Africa and in any particular shape or form of our part of that spirit or atmosphere." This also include the few blacks who, he points out, are also isolated from their white fellows, while both sections are being influenced by "European ideas" consolidated by the influx of the international print and the marvelous magazines and art books. Likewise, "in the mid-sixties a small group of professional black artists began to express their reactions to township life in a strong 'German expressionist' manner, using conte chalk as a medium," while, on the theoretical and ideological level we assume, the "application of international ideas to our situation has clouded our artistic insight." All these he says, have contributed to the "spiritual bankruptcy that seems to be establishing itself in our art."

But "European ideas" need not necessarily detract from the merit of artistic creations or its national character, and certainly the success of the revolution does not mean the jettisoning of worthwhile cultural acquirements, theoretical or material, in order to return to "a folk art of consequence" which Mr. Skotnes longs for.

The absence of stimulation among artists might not be mainly historical, as Cecil Skotnes claims, and it need not be "international ideas" which cloud artistic insight, although he does not identify these ideas; nor need it mean that these artists are necessarily oblivious of or unaffected by the revolutionary situation referred to. Certainly the oppressed black majority are far from pessimistic, both in their political and artistic resistance. But believing that all artists, plastic and literary alike, must entertain a broad-minded outlook, albeit on varying levels, it is not difficult to imagine the dilemma of those who belong to the ruling racial minority in South Africa.

The black artist in South Africa is not averse to mixing his work with "politics;" he cannot but accept that as one of the victims of the oppressive society, his work almost automatically becomes involved, even if merely to "record our times" as Mr. Skotnes wants art to do.

For us or the conscious artist, man is not made for the sabbath, but the sabbath for man—society is not made for the artist, but the artist for society. The function of art is to assist the development of man's consciousness, to help improve society.

Others of course emphatically reject this standpoint. Art is an *aim* in itself and to convert it into a *means* of achieving any extraneous aim, even the most noble, is to lower the dignity of creative production.

Those who have been raised in the school of the bourgeoisie

easily cling to such conceptions. On the other hand, considering that it is impossible for everybody to be of like mind, it is not difficult to imagine that there are artists in South Africa who are by no means in agreement with the course taken by their society and are embarrassed by it. The artist's relations with the ruling sphere may be a source of great vexation to him. But unable to accept the so-called utilitarian view of art, that is the tendency to attach to artistic productions the function of judging and phenomena of life, he chooses to ignore life, society, altogether. At best this might mean "art for art's sake," and adopting this theory is an easy way out; the ivory tower is a refuge from the slings and arrows of an outrageous society.

For any intelligent and sensitive person, life in the South African racist atmosphere might be a distressing experience. The general callousness of his community and the forbidding stare of the oppressed must frighten the sensitive white artist in particular. Rather than paint the ugly face of his racist community he turns to the natural beauty of the land, and he finds in this so-called tranquil atmosphere an avenue of escape.

But we have seen that even the most tightly fortified white laager cannot ignore the effects the upsurge of the revolutionary black people forever, if at all. The life of the black people cannot ever be separated from the social environment as a whole, and so the artist inside the laager too must take cogniscance of the cultural manifestations of this upsurge.

The development of the revolutionary struggle is a most important characteristic of the South African scene today, and not even the practice of apartheid or the police state can separate experiences which can be shared, however difficult, across the barriers. Skotnes says that through "limited confrontation between a few artists and the reality of our time some anger has resulted, but here again it is the writer who has led .... " Then it is the writers who are more in touch with reality and this is demonstrated by their general concern with social and political problems. It must mean that all the complaints and observations made by Cecil Skotnes about the failure of painters and sculptors being unaffected by developments in South Africa, must hinge largely on their ignorance or lack of awareness of reality. Sensitivity is one thing, but to demonstrate this sensitivity positively is another. "Art for art's sake" arises essentially where the artist is out of harmony with his social environment, but the millions of black people are also part of the South African picture and the beauty of the African landscape is no substitute for the dynamism of their life and struggles.

Undoubtedly the momentum of the revolutionary struggle will drag many more artists from their ivory towers to force them to come out on one side or the other. Though he himself queries "what events will check the spiritual bankruptcy," Cecil Skotnes passes his own judgment on his guilty colleagues: "The key to a meaningful art that will record our time lies in the spirit of the artist—in his humanity and his intellectual honesty. And if the times have little influence on an artist's work, especially such momentous times, he should seek a new profession."

Paul Robeson and Africa

Paul Robeson, the African American singer, has been a hero for all black South Africans. In his rich, baritone voice, with deep messages of hope, many oppressed South Africans have taken heart. Furthermore, Robeson represents the high achievement that blacks in South Africa have often associated with white success. A few South Africans, the writer Peter Abrahams being among them, had the honor of meeting Robeson during his lifetime. Alex La Guma often spoke longingly and regretfully about not having been fortunate enough to meet Robeson while he was alive. In this 1971 address to a general audience in the former German Democratic Republic, La Guma sings not only the praise of Robeson, but he ties together the struggle of the African American and African people, as well as the struggling oppressed all over the world.

H onored chairman, friends, allow me to express my sincere thanks to you and the organizers of this symposium on Paul Robeson and on the struggle of the Afro-American people, for the invitation to be present here. We can well understand the sentiments which stimulated this gathering. The cause of Afro-Asian solidarity; solidarity with the Afro-American people, and in fact with all oppressed and persecuted people throughout the world, is a characteristic of the German Democratic Republic (GDR). Since its inception, the GDR has done many things which has vindicated the honor of progressive Germany. Your people have risen like the phoenix from the ashes of Nazism; and you have shown time and again that the spirit of Thaelmann, Beimler, the Spartacists, Karl Marx and Frederick Engels did not die as a result of the Hitlerite depredations.

The present demonstration of your solidarity with the Afro-

American people whose suffering and heroism is today epitomized by Angela Davis, is certainly close to the hearts of the African people as well.

The forefathers of the Afro-American people were brought from my continent during the seventeenth century. The black people of the United States are there today because their ancestors were brought there against their will, chained and bound in the dark holds of slave ships. From free man to second-class citizen, the struggle of our peoples have always been towards the same objective: complete freedom.

The newly captured Africans who leaped from the slave ships to their deaths; the young Afro-Americans facing the might of white supremacy on the streets of the United States; the heroism of Angela Davis, are all common factors in the long and bloody history of the black man's constant efforts to free himself from the yoke of slavery.

The struggle of the Afro-American parallels in many ways the struggles of colonial peoples all over the world to rid themselves of exploiters and slave-masters. Dr. Martin Luther King murdered in Tennessee for the same reasons Patrice Lumumba was murdered in the Congo—and by the same forces. The African black man and the American black man are fighting the common enemy, international imperialism, whether in the form of Portuguese and South African racist troops in southern Africa or the police forces of the United States. In Vietnam and Indochina the same struggle goes on against the same enemy for the same reasons.

While we wage our present-day struggle, we must recall at some time or other the struggles of the past as well. We Africans who today confront the forces of fascism and racist oppression call all the time on the international progressive community for unity and support for our cause. The international alliance of solidarity with oppressed Africa has a history in which the contribution of progressive America has a place. Not only is Paul Robeson close to us because of his ancestral origins, but because he stands great in the long struggle of the American people, both black and white, for justice both in his homeland and outside it.

Although of African descent Paul Robeson did not come in contact with the cause of African freedom until the end of the 1920s. It was in 1928 that he placed the song "Ole Man River" on the musical map of the world. He had come to London then to appear in "Show Boat." It is perhaps typical of a man from an oppressed community to feel more at home among others in the same plight, rather than in the company of the celebrities who feted him in London. So Paul Robeson felt much easier when in the company of British dockworkers and Welsh miners, and the many Africans whom he met. Many of the Africans in London then were students and political workers, and from these Paul Robeson found a revival of Africa within him. Among the Africans he met in London then were several who were to become noteworthy afterwards—men like Jomo Kenyatta, Kwane Nkrumah and others.

It might be of interest to take a quick glance at what was happening in Africa at that time. It was a period when more and more efforts were being made by the colonialists to extract the maximum of wealth from Africa in order to bolster up their tottering economy. Law upon law, regulation on regulation were introduced in the regions of East and West Africa to ensure the maximum cheap labor and the highest production of raw materials and other wealth.

In Tanganyika, for example, an unwarranted departure from work was considered a criminal offense; in Uganda regulations enforced every adult African to work for thirty days a year without wages on road construction. Peasants were allowed to sell their crops only within a fixed time in restricted zones and for set prices. The policies of the imperialists transformed the countries of Africa into hell for the Africans and paradise for all foreign exploiters.

Increased exploitation coincided with social and political awareness among Africans and they were inevitably drawn into the anti-imperialist movement. In 1920 the Kikuyu of Kenya set up their first organization; in Tanganyika the establishment of mass peasants' and workers' organizations was a sign of the growing awareness of the working people; in Dahomey in West Africa railway workers launched a significant strike, the first of its kind; likewise, workers took action in Senegal, Guinea, and on the Ivory Coast. These were the first efforts of the modern working-class and political movements in Africa.

The Kikuyu Central Association sent its secretary general, Jomo Kenyatta, to Britain where he carried on intensive work on behalf of the African population of Kenya. It is under these circumstances that Paul Robeson had the opportunity to come into contact with the African situation. Through these contacts, through the inevitable discussions, Robeson became aware of the continent of his ancestors who had been taken from it in chains.

In what was then the Union of South Africa, a rapid consciousness of the importance of the national liberation struggle of the African people there was also developing at that time. Together with the demands of the oppressed black people for emancipation, a class-consciousness was also taking deep root. African workers saw themselves not only oppressed as black people, but also exploited as workers. Inevitably the ideas of socialism caught the interest of more and more Africans.

It is not coincidental that the visit to the Soviet Union by Paul Robeson in 1934 had the same effect on him as it did on the South African leader Joseph Gumede. Paul Robeson on visiting the Soviet Union said that he had seen whole nations of so-called "primitive peoples" now building highly developed socialist republics, working and building countless new factories, schools, universities, all within twenty years. To him this proved the falsity of the colonialist claim that black people would not be able to rule themselves for thousands of years.

Gumede, a leader of the African National Congress, told a mass meeting of Africans when he returned from the Soviet Union: "I have seen the new world to come, where it has already begun.

I have been to the new Jerusalem." He claimed that he had brought the key which would unlock the door to freedom.

Paul Robeson, the singer, after those days placed his voice and his talent at the service of the struggle for emancipation of the black oppressed, and at the service of all progressive mankind. He was an artist who did not see art in isolation from the problems which beset society, the whole world, the whole of humanity. Becoming more and more aware of the problems of the Afro-American and African people, he was endowed with the wisdom to see the link between black oppression and the rest of the world's problems. It was therefore inevitable that he was drawn into the worldwide antifascist struggle of the 1930s and subsequent years.

Caught in the whirlpool of the fight to destroy fascism—a fight that was both dramatic and horrible—it was at this time that he saw clearly that he as an artist, a singer, a man of talent could not possibly stand aloof from the future of humanity. He saw that the artist who was honest could never belong in an ivory tower while mankind was engaged in one of the titanic struggles of its history.

I think that his outlook as an artist is significantly illustrated by a speech made in London's Albert Hall at a rally in support of the Spanish republic, and reported in the South African anti-imperialist magazine, *The Liberator*, in 1937. Paul Robeson said then:

> Every artist, every scientist, must decide now where he stands. He has no alternative. There is no standing above the conflict on Olympian heights.... The battlefield is everywhere, there is no sheltered rear.... Fascism fights to destroy the culture which society has created; created through pain and suffering, through desperate toil, but with unconquerable will and lofty vision.... What matters a man's profession or vocation? Fascism is no respecter of persons. It makes no distinction between combatants and non-combatants.... The artist must take sides; he must

elect to fight for freedom or for slavery. I have made my choice. I have no alternative. The history of the capitalist era is characterized by the degradation of my people; despoiled of their lands, their women ravished, their culture destroyed.... I say the true artist cannot hold himself aloof. The legacy of culture from our predecessors is in danger. It is the foundation upon which we build a still more lofty edifice. It belongs not only to us, not only to the present generation—it belongs to posterity and must be defended to the death.

These words of Paul Robeson hold good today as they did then.

It was in 1937 that he also helped to found the Council for African Affairs of which he became chairman. This American organization had two main aims: to support the cause of African freedom, collecting funds for various African causes, and also to tell Americans the truth about affairs and events in Africa. Under the first of the council's objectives, the people of South Africa remember the assistance provided during a severe famine in the eastern part of our country shortly after the Second World War. However, the other aims of the Council provided the opportunity for many Americans to learn the truth about our country. Until then I believe that most Americans thought in terms of Edgar Rice Burroughs' stories of Tarzan and the apes whenever they heard the continent of Africa mentioned.

The South African people also remember with appreciation and affection Paul Robeson's first task when he was released from the United States after the McCarthy persecutions. In 1958, just arrived in Europe from the United States, he sang in a special service at St. Paul's Cathedral London in aid of the fund for the defense of South African political prisoners.

As a South African I believe I can say with truth that Paul Robeson had a special spot within himself for my country. We recall that in 1950 when workers were shot down by the fascist

police at a May Day demonstration, Paul Robeson addressed a
meeting of the National Labor Conference for Negro Rights, telling
his audience:

"Twelve South African workers now lie dead, shot in a peace-
ful demonstration by Malan's fascist police; as silent testimony to
the fact that ... it is later than they think in the procession of
history, and that rich land must one day return to Africans on
whose backs the proud skyscrapers of the Johannesburg rich were
built .... "

Today the South African people stand on the threshold of the
final struggle for the liberation of the black majority and the other
oppressed communities. In 1961 the armed struggle for the overthrow of fascism in South Africa was begun; for the overthrow of
white supremacy, of injustice, of racial hatred and the exploitation
of our hard-pressed people. In 1967 the first battalions of our
partisan fighters met the racist troops of South Africa and Rhode-
sia. Our people have died there in the beautiful Zambesi Valley,
since they have said that they no longer wish to lay down their
lives defenselessly. I do not think that the South African movement
today claims wholesale success or that victory will come soon. But
we have reached the turning point in our history, and we have no
doubt that victory will be ours.

Very recently Richard Nixon, President of the United States,
claimed that he and his government are against apartheid and
racism in South Africa: "Racism is abhorrent to my administration
and to me personally. We cannot be indifferent to apartheid." This
is a lie. In the first place the ruling class of the United States cannot
be against racism in South Africa and at the same time condone
and encourage it in the United States. Secondly, the United States
of America is the second biggest foreign investor in South Africa
and millions of dollars in profits are being sucked from the marrow
and blood of African exploitation in South Africa.

We South Africans know full well who are our friends and
allies in the United States. They are people like Paul Robeson who

has raised his voice in song and worked in the interest of solidarity with the South African people. They are people like the late Martin Luther King, W. E. B. Du Bois, and Angela Davis and all the Afro-Americans and genuine democrats fighting for the cause of justice, freedom and humanity in their country.

PART THREE

On a Wedding Day

In 1964, Alex La Guma's second novel, *And a Threefold Cord*, was published in Berlin. The novel deals with the oppressed blacks who live in slum dwellings in Cape Town. The extract "On A Wedding Day" was meant originally to be a short story. La Guma left it in its story form, but later transformed the story into a novel. In this extract, the writer describes in detail the house and slum area where the wedding is to occur.

Ma Pauls rose earlier than usual that morning. She left the sagging wrought-iron and brass-knobbed double-bed, and went out into the front room of the corrugated-iron house, carrying a candle. She was a small woman, thickened by childbirth, with a kindly face and eyes that could change quickly from geniality to sternness. The knot in her greying hair had come undone and hung in an untidy tangle in her neck. She wore a shapeless old night-dress and she had thick brown arms.

In the front room of the house there was a smell of cake and pastry. The old oval-topped table had been laid the previous night, and in its center stood the small white wedding cake under its protective veil of net material that kept off the flies; while around it were arrayed plates of tiny tarts and tea cakes, big coconut tarts, jam tarts and decorated fruit cakes. Bottles of soft drinks stood like sentinels among the display. From the plywood-and-cardboard ceiling, colored paper streamers hung remotely in the light of the candle.

Ma Pauls went to the window and drew aside the curtain. It was a new curtain, hung the day before, and beyond it the sky in the east was greying slowly with the cautious light that comes with the early morning.

The light was pale and clean, and the rest of the sky was still dark except for the scattered confetti of stars.

"Well," Ma said softly. "It's going to be a nice day." She said this with a quiet pleasure, and having made the prophecy, went out of the room to the kitchen. There, using the candle flame, she lit the big lamp that hung from a beam in the cardboard ceiling.

The floor of the kitchen sagged, and there was an iron Sheffield stove in the fireplace next to the dresser. Against the wall under the window beyond the fireplace was a wooden single-bed. Charlie Pauls slept on it, one arm trailing onto the floor, his mouth open. He had a lean,sharp-boned face with stubble like coal dust over it, and short kinky hair.

The clang of the stove lid awoke him and he said sleepily: "Ma?"

"It's early yet," Ma said. "But we got a big day in front of us."

Charlie sat up in the bed and yawned hugely. He swung his feet onto the floor and reached for his dungarees.

Ma said, "You get that tin full so we can have some bath water for Jessie and your Dad. I don't know about Oupa, he hasn't had a bath since Ouma died, I reckon, and I don't think he's going to start afresh today. And I think you could have one, too," she added.

"Hell. I bathed yesterday, Ma."

"Awright. Go and get that tin full."

Charlie fastened the buttons of his old cord shirt, and picked up the scoured four-gallon can from the shelf. He unlatched the kitchen door and went out.

Back in the bedroom, Ma paused at the battered wardrobe with its cracked mirror and loose-hinged door from which a wooden hanger suspended the bridal dress of cheap white satin, laced and flounced. She touched the smooth material with rough hands, conjuring up memories. With the dress would go the veil she herself had worn.

In the wooden single-bed, opposite the big brass-knobbed one in which Dad Pauls snuffled and grunted in his sleep, the girl Jessica woke up and peered thick-eyed over the edge of the blankets.

"Is it time awready, Ma?" she asked sleepily.

"Hush," the mother said. "Sleep on. It's early yet, I'll call you when is time to get up, child."

Dad Pauls turned and snorted in the big bed. In another wedged into a corner, the grandfather purred and whistled like a boiling kettle.

Later the fire was growling in the kitchen, and the bath-water-tin vibrating gently on the stove next to the big pot of porridge.

Behind the stars the sky greyed steadily, so that soon the stars were absorbed by the growing light and all along the horizon there was a spray of red and orange dyeing the thin, scattered clouds into frayed ribbons of color. Roosters crowed among the shacks, and the brown shepherd mongrel whose name was Redskin loped easily into the Pauls' yard and entered the kitchen.

"Get that hound from under my feet," Ma said. "He's just a nuisance every time."

"Out, Redskin. Out," Charlie Pauls said, patting the dog.

Ma was setting out the chipped enamel breakfast plates when Dad Pauls came into the kitchen. He was tall, thin and elderly, with a lined face, and calloused and gnarled hands like pieces of old leather. He was wearing long underwear, and scratched his armpits as he came in.

He said, "where's my clothes, Ma? Did you iron my shirt?" He had a gruff voice, and sounded irritable.

"Now reckon for you," Ma replied sternly. "There's lots to do before you put on your suit, man. Put on yesterday's clothes so long. Then come and eat."

"What you mean, lots to do?" Dad asked. "We been busy all blerry day yesterday."

"Never min' what's to do," Ma told him. "There's plenty.

Now go and put on them old clothes."

Dad went out again in his baggy longs, grumbling.

"I hope Ronny's car is okay," Ma said to Charlie.

"I'll go down and see him later," Charlie told her. "It ought to be awright."

"I hope so. It broke down that time he took us to Stellenbosch. And wanted ten bob for petrol, too."

"Ah, don't worry so, Ma," Charlie said. "The car'll be okay. You see."

"And your Uncle Ben. I bet he'll turn up besotted."

"Man, Ma. Uncle Ben will be okay."

Ma ladled porridge into the plates on the kitchen table. "I don't trust your Uncle Ben much," she complained.

Dad Pauls came into the kitchen again. He had put on a set of tattered overalls. Behind him came Oupa Pauls, the grandfather, as tall and thin as his son, but stooped slightly, his face shrewd and bony, with eyes as evil as a child's eyes. He had a scrubby grey beard over the lower part of his dark brown face, and tufts of grey hair like pieces of dirty, unravelled cottonwool, protruding from his large ears.

"Good morning, children," he cried in his cracked voice. "Are we ready for what the Lord provides?"

"Sit, old man," Ma told him. And to Dad, "Is Jessie still asleep?"

"*Ja.* All the time."

"Let her sleep," Ma said, as they all sat down. "Soon's we finished with things I can see to her."

Charlie scattered sugar over his porridge, and said grinning. "Well, she won't get much sleep tonight."

"Charlie Pauls," Ma said, eyeing him sternly. "I don't want that kind of talk by my table."

"Okay, Ma," Charlie said, smiling at his plate.

"People, we better say grace," Oupa said.

He bowed his head, and the others bowed their heads, and

Oupa said, "The Lord give us this food, and we thank him for it. The Lord provides and there'll never a person be hungry so long he trust in the Lord. Amen."

"Amen," Ma said.

Ma said, "We got things to do." Pa crammed his mouth, growling, and Ma went on: "Charlie, you and Dad got to kill those fowls. The two black hens and the *kapokkie*. I got to have everything ready before we go down to the church. Mrs. Isaacs and Titty will be coming to help just now. Charlie can pluck the fowls while Dad . . . . "

"I want to go down and see Ronny get the car in order, *mos*," Charlie broke in, hoping to avoid any excess duty.

"I thought you said the car is okay," Ma said suspiciously.

"Well I just want to see he gets here in time," Charlie explained.

"Awright," Ma said. "Dad and Oupa can do the fowls. I'll have hot water on. Then I can see to Jessie, too, while they're busy. She got to have a bath. I'm not going to have her smelling like that fish factory on her wedding day."

Dad said, hesitantly: "Ma, you reckon we kind of can have a little *doppie* after we finished with the fowls, likely?"

"No drinking until after church," Ma stated flatly.

"Just one round, Ma," Dad urged.

"After church. You can't go into church with a drink in." To Charlie, Ma said: "And you better go around by Uncle Ben on your way. See *he's* in order. I bet he had a good few last night. Friday, *mos*."

"Okay," Charlie said.

"And don't stay a whole year," the mother said. "Oupa, you can go and sit outside until it's time to go. We don't need you."

"I hope the minister got a good tex'," Oupa said.

"There isn't a tex' by a wedding," Charlie said, getting up from the table. "They just marry you."

Now that breakfast was over, a little fever struck them all, and they were infected with a strong desire for this day.

Ma started at the stove, while the three men went out into the yard.

The day had come fully now, and there was a warm light on the hard surface of the yard, and on the weeds that sprung through the trodden, pottery-hard soil. There was a fig tree in the yard, and an old mulberry tree with spindly branches like the arms of the aged. Around the house were other shacks scattered among the growths of portjackson wattle and old pines.

Dad and Oupa and Charlie Pauls went down to the chicken run at the end of the yard. Dad carried the worn butcher knife, well whetted, in one hand. The poultry, as if sensing danger, set up a squawking and crowing as the three men approached, fleeing around the run and scrabbling against the enclosing wire. Charlie opened the gate and climbed into the run. Oupa and Dad watched him.

"Grab the red one, Charles," Dad said. "That one with the blind left eye."

"Ma said the two blacks," Charlie said, watching the chickens warily.

"The red's got a lot of meat on her," Dad advised.

"She's a good layer," Oupa put in. "She's a good layer. We get a lot of eggs from her. She'll lay more, too."

But Dad was adamant. He said, "Leave the one black layer, and we'll butcher the other and that red. Go on, man, Charlie."

"Well, awright," Charlie said, and pounced on the red hen.

After a while they each held a captive bird, holding them where the wings joined the back, while they screeched and kicked. The three men walked with the sacrificial birds to the kitchen door, by the step of which Ma had placed a big iron basin.

Dad laid his bird in the basin, holding it down, and Charlie gave the red hen to Oupa to hold in his free hand, and squatted to help Dad.

Charlie cleared the fowl's neck, and Dad butchered it quickly and skillfully, the warm blood spurting over their hands while the dying carcass thrashed and jerked. Oupa passed the others and Dad called out to the kitchen, "Bring the hot water, Ma."

Oupa and Dad plucked the chickens quickly, running their fingers through the feathers to loosen them, plucking them out swiftly before they tightened in the skin.

Charlie walked over to the tap and washed blood from his hands. "Well, I must go down and see Uncle Ben and *ou* Ronny," he said. He was anxious to get away from the routine chores, and do something important.

"Awright," Ma said from the kitchen door. "You see that Ben turn up. An' he better make a blerry good spitch."

"He will make the speech, Ma," Charlie said. "I hope to God that chorchy Jessie's going to marry, turn up."

"You get on," Ma told him, admonishingly. "You got no right to talk like that about Alfie." And she added, as if giving her final approval, "He is a nice boy-*tjie*."

Charlie walked along the dusty street that staggered between the scattered rows of shanties. Down the street were ruts which the woodman's wagon and battered cars had cut, like lines of age on the face of the hard mud. In the weed-ridden lots washing began to appear, stirring like festive bunting on the strung wires. Chickens and deputations of mongrel dogs were everywhere, here and there the sounds of axes splitting wood, and the voices of children. Women carrying shopping bags trailed towards the distant main road and the oasis of stores.

Charlie Pauls found his Uncle Ben in the sand lot behind his cabin. Uncle Ben was short and paunchy, with bristly hair, the color of steel-wool, combed stiffly back from the balding forehead that curved away from his dark brown eyes with blood-shot veins in the whites. He wore a clean white shirt without a necktie, and navy-blue trousers.

He said, smiling: "Hullo, Charlieboy, howsit, *ou man*?"

"Okay, Uncle Ben. Came down to see was you ready."

"It's early yet," Uncle Ben said. "I got a basket of a headache, too." He winked, smiling again. "But I got up early for this day. Could have slept on, but I got up early. *Ja, boetis.*" He asked, "You like a *doppie*? Still got one can put by."

Charlie licked his lips, smiling back. "Well, we might as well get into the mood, hey, Uncle?"

Uncle Ben laughed softly, and went into the house. He came out after a moment, carrying a half-gallon jar of white wine by the ring at its neck, and two glasses in the fingers of his other hand. They sat on the rough bench against the back wall of the cabin and Uncle Ben poured the glasses full.

"Again so," Uncle Ben said, drinking.

"First for the day," Charlie said. "Old lady wouldn't let us take a drink until after the church. Remember you got to make that speech, Uncle Ben."

Uncle Ben sighed as he emptied his glass. He said, "*Ja.* That speech. Wonder why your Ma pick me for that speech."

"Well, youse her oldest brother, *mos*," Charlie said. "Also, you belong *mos* to the lodge. Lodge people always making speeches."

"That's no reason for your Ma, Charlie," Uncle Ben frowned. "Ma always talked about my drinking. Call me a blerry *dronklap*, a drunky. Never could tolerate a drinking man. Your Dad don't drink too much, and Oupa could make a real church-like speech. That *ou* boy is full of the Jesus it comes out his ears. No." He shook his head. "Ma don't give a damn I belong to the lodge or anything."

"Man, Ma's awright," Charlie said. "Ma said once, 'man isn't so bad he can't do no good.' Talk funny sometimes."

"I was bestman for your Ma's wedding," Uncle Ben said, reminiscently, as the level of the wine dropped in the jar. "She looked nice. Your Ouma, God bless her soul, cried like a bogger. Oupa will want a Bible speech. I'm not good at Bible speeches. Maybe it is because I got too much of the devil."

"Well," Charlie said. "You got to make that devil work like

hell this afternoon. We better not take any more drinks. You got to be on your feet come the time to make that speech."

"Well, just one more, man."

"Okay, then. Last one, hey? I got to go down to Ronny to see that he got that jalopy fix up."

"I'll go down with you," Uncle Ben said, pouring the glasses full again. "I can think about the speech while we walk."

"Awright, *ou* Ben," Charlie said, feeling merrily tipsy.

"You reckon we can just have one more, hey?" Uncle Ben said. "I move in that direction."

Charlie hesitated for a moment, then said: "I seconds the motion, Mister Chairman."

"Agreed, un-un-unanimissly," Uncle Ben cried. "Just like a blerry lodge meeting."

When the wine had reached three inches from the bottom of the jar, they decided to leave. Uncle Ben slipped the jar over the doorstep, pulled the door shut and locked it. Then they left the yard, lurching a little.

They did not use the street, but crossed other lots and back-yards, kicking up powdery dust as they walked, saluting people who saw them, and discoursing together.

"It's got to be a real nice wedding speech," Uncle Ben was saying. "I reckon I'll start like this." He paused to gather his breath. "Friends, we garrer here togeddar on this great day because why these children been join togerrar in holy mattermony . . . . " He shook the steel-wool head, and wiped his mouth on the back of his hand. "Don't sound right, man."

Uncle Ben circled the battered car. It had been washed down, and its paint was clean. A long time ago the top of the Dodge had been cut off with a cold chisel, and converted into something like an open tourer. The upholstery was torn and patched, and the windscreen badly jaundiced.

"Hell, she's awright, man," Ronny said. He spat-spat-spatted the side of the car with the flat of his hand. "Just a springleaf cracked, and something wrong with the ignition and the carburetor, you know, hey."

He lowered the hood and snapped the catches tight.

"Oh, God," said Charlie.

"Don't worry, pally," Ronny assured him, smiling. "She'll go awright. We have to swing her, though. That's all, man." He eyed the two. "Well, you *jubas* look like you real ready for the wedding."

"Uncle Ben here's got to make the speech," Charlie said. "We got to get up there in time. Ma and Jessie will be on their nerves. True as fat."

"I'll wash up and get dressed then," Ronny said.

"How's you Ma, Ronnyboy?" Uncle Ben asked.

"Gone shopping. She'll be coming up afterwards." He walked over to the house. "You wan't to come inside?"

"No, man," Uncle Ben said. "I'll stay out here and think over that speech." He sat down on the running-board of the car and sighed; and now there was an air of concentration about him. Charlie sat down by him and picked up a twig and idly drew lines in the dust between his feet.

"Wedding speech is something special," Uncle Ben said. "Man and woman ought to get married only once, so's to make it special. Like your Ma and Dad. *Ja.* Got to be something special."

"You ever make a special speech before?" Charlie asked.

"No, man. All the speeches I ever made was ornery likely. Reading of minutes and matters arising and stuff like that. One year I had to give the secketerry's report."

"And I thought lodge was so importan'."

"Was kind of importan'," Uncle Ben said. "But I left it after some years. Blerry thing wasn't going nowhere. Now I got a problem."

"Well," Charlie said. "I hope you do it okay. Ma'll kick your backside, you don't make that speech nice. She's blerry suspicious about you awready."

Uncle Ben sighed. He said anxiously, "I'm a little on my nerves. Think I ought to have another *dop*. We'll have one when we go up to pick up my jacket."

*   *   *   *   *

Oupa and Dad Pauls had put on their navy-blue suits, neatly pressed and creased, and white shirts, and their boots were well-polished so that you could not see the scuff-marks on the toe-caps, and the worn welts cleverly disguised with blacking, so that their age became undetectable. The suits were special suits, carefully preserved and worn only on particular occasions, like church services or funerals.

Now there was a tension throughout the house. For having dressed, all were now eager to leave. Ma Pauls wore her Sunday duster coat over the new floral dress, and a straw hat like a man's boater, only it was black and anchored to her head with a pin decorated with a large red cherry in wax.

But Charlie had not arrived, and his black suit was laid out on the bed in Ma's room, together with his shirt with the cutaway collar which he had bought on the pay-by system especially for this day. He had bought a gray necktie, too, and his grey cotton gloves were folded neatly on top of the suit.

In the front room, the daughter, Jessie, sat in her bridal array of satin and lace veil. She had been carefully placed in the room, out of harm's way, like a piece of delicate china to be preserved until the rare occasion came when it could be moved. She was something special that day: a showpiece, a mystery, a shrine.

And there was tension within her, too. And a small fear and an anxiety. So that she bit her lips and sat with lowered eyes, as if to look up would reveal the beating of her heart.

Then, at last, they all heard the shattering detonations of Ronny's Dodge as it pulled up outside the house, and the tension dropped like a discarded dish-rag, and Ma said: "Well, is about time."

Charlie went around the back of the house and through the kitchen to the bedroom where his clothes waited. He did not wish to face Ma now that he had kept them all waiting, knowing that when she saw him dressed and ready, some of the anger would subside. So he washed hurriedly in the porcelain basin on the old dresser, and pulled on the shirt with the cutaway collar, and finally the black suit. He had a new belt, too, a thin strap of tooled leather with a buckle decorated with silver steer-horns.

When, when he emerged onto the sagging verandah where they all waited, with the aroma of roasted chicken and spiced rice behind them, Charlie was spruced and combed, the grey tie neatly knotted and his gloves held delicately in one hand. There was a hint of inflammation in his eyes.

But Ma watched him suspiciously, and then looked to where Uncle Ben sat in the front of the open Dodge, his face hang-dog and his eyes puffed and sheepish. Uncle Ben wore a striped navy-blue suit, shiny with wear, but pressed, and a black necktie, and his hands worried a new, hard, brown hat with a little gaudy feather stuck in the band. He did not look at Ma, but sat there, waiting for the storm to break over him.

But Ma said nothing, and made no sound except for a disparaging sniff as she turned away.

Oupa Pauls said impatiently, in his guitar-string voice: "Lord, when we going? When we going?"

In the street before the house, and along the sagging, warped fences, neighbors had gathered to watch. Children pushed between the grownups, or crouched and peered through the gaps in the peeled-branch poles. There was a fine current of excitement coursing tensely through the little crowd, and then when the family on the verandah parted and Jessie appeared, a drawn-out sigh went up and a murmur of pleasure broke from the spectators and rippled gently among them.

Jessie stood for a moment on the verandah, her eyes downcast and a flush upon her face beneath the veil, her gloved hands holding the bouquet of new lilies against her stomach. She stood like that, hesitant, shy: quivering, until Ma said quietly, "Well, get along child."

She walked down the verandah step with Jessie, Charlie coming behind, grinning with the courage of wine. Behind him came Dad and Oupa, the old man's face cracked with pleasure.

The women who had volunteered to prepare for the homecoming after the ceremony, were near, and Ma said to them: "Don't put the water on for the tea now, ladies. Tea's in the tin on the shelf by the kitchen door. But I think we must wait till everybody's back before we start dishing up. You can cut the cake on the dresser so long."

When the women had trooped onto the verandah, Ma took command of the family.

"Jessie, you sit in the back, and Oupa and Dad each side of you. Don't crush that dress, hey. Oupa, you and Dad be careful. Don't mess her up." She glared at Uncle Ben. "I'll sit with Ben. Charlie, you think you can squeeze in between me and Ronny?"

"Easy, Ma," Charlie replied, glad that he was out of the line of her corrosive glare.

Dad said, "What about Winnie? We got to pick up Winnie, the bridesmaid."

"We'll make place for her," Ma told him.

Then they were all in the car, except Ronny. Oupa and Dad sat rigidly in the back, their taut bodies held carefully away from Jessie who tingled with anxiety on the cracked upholstery. Uncle Ben sat, not looking at Ma, his face troubled and his mind clicking and rattling like a stale peanut as he wrestled desperately with the words of the speech which he was trying to memorize. He belched suddenly, and covered his mouth quickly with a hand, while Ma, catching the smell of the white wine, sneered. Beside her, Charlie felt a sudden sorrow for the discomfort of Uncle Ben.

"You all ready?" Ronny called from where he stood by the

radiator of the Dodge.

A look of shock passed over Ma's face and she cried: "No. Not yet. *Wag. Wag.* Wait. Wait." They all stared at her. "The ribbon," she said, excitedly. "I forgot the ribbon." She turned to the women on the verandah and called to one of them. "Grace. Gracie. The ribbon. Look on the dressing-table in my bedroom. The ribbon, man." The woman dashed into the house.

"Ma. Ma. It's almost time," Charlie cried. And Dad said, "And what is it now, woman?"

Their impatience caught the crowd of watchers, too, like a minor plague, and another murmur splashed from them like a muted cry of despair. And even Jessie asked, "What is it, Ma?"

"Never seen a wedding without ribbon on the car," Ma told them firmly. "Got to have a ribbon on the car."

"How, Ma," Charlie said. "We'll be late."

"*Humph*," the mother sniffed, and snapped a look at Uncle Ben. "I remember *other* people making *me* late for *my* wedding. A' Uncle of yours *mos* lost his gloves. Held up the business for a whole half-hour."

Uncle Ben crouched miserably under the dragon-like stare. But then the woman darted from the house, holding aloft a roll of white satin ribbon, and Ma said, happily: "There's it. Got to have a ribbon. Ronny, you fix it, hey?"

"Okay, Ma Pauls."

Ronny took the ribbon, and coming around, tied one end of it to the metal framework of the yellow-brown-stained windshield, and went back, unrolling the satin, and then twisting it around the decorative figure on the radiator-cap. Then he fastened the other end of the ribbon to the opposite wide of the windscreen.

"There she is," he said, and Ma nodded in satisfaction, and the ribbon ran taut and white and shiny in a long V over the bonnet of the car.

"Okay," Ronny said. "Now let's go." He grinned at them and stooped, clutched the crankhandle and swung. He swung again, and again, panting a little. And then the ignition caught and the old engine sprang into life with a shattering blast as the pistons lunged and roared, wracking the battered frame so that the car shook and trembled as if with palsy. The tearing clamor quietened, until what was left was a throbbing, vibrating rattle. Ronny came around to the wheel door, smiling triumphantly, slapping the scarred surface of the engine cover with affection, as if he knew that the old car understood his pleasure.

He climbed in behind the wheel, slamming the door shut, and settled down, working the gears jerkily. Then a small cheer went up from the crowd as the car lurched away, and Ronny cried, "I'll drive her slow, so there won't be no dust."

Index